HISTORY OF THE UNITED STATES

TOLD IN ONE SYLLABLE WORDS

BY

MISS JOSEPHINE POLLARD

WITH ILLUSTRATIONS

APPLEWOOD BOOKS

CARLISLE, MASSACHUSETTS

*History of The United States
Told in One Syllable Words*
was first published in 1884

COLUMBUS DISCOVERING AMERICA.

THE

HISTORY

OF THE

UNITED STATES:

TOLD IN

ONE SYLLABLE WORDS

BY

MISS JOSEPHINE POLLARD.

WITH COLORED ILLUSTRATIONS.

NEW YORK:
McLOUGHLIN BROTHERS, PUBLISHERS.

A FEW WORDS.

THIS is a tale in short words for small folks, on the way our land grew. There is much that all boys and girls ought to know, of the brave deeds of our great men.

To read this will make you want to read more and to learn more, of what the men of old times and of new times did to make our land the great land it now is.

The men of old times fought to make the land free. We who live in this day should be proud to have it free, and do our best to keep it so.

All young folks should be glad to learn of the land in which they live; to know who were its chief men; and to tell of the wars which were fought, in which the foes of the land were put to flight. They should know, too, what a bright and glad thing it is that we now have peace in the land, after all the wars we have been through.

God has led us on through ways that have been strange, to reach the place where we now stand. The men of all the earth look on our land, and we are glad to have them call it

THE LAND OF THE FREE

and

THE HOME OF THE BRAVE.

CONTENTS.

HISTORY OF THE UNITED STATES.

CHAPTER I.

THE NORTH MEN.

IN the North of Europe lived the North, or Norse men, who were fond of the sea. They were a large, strong race. They wore the skins of wild beasts for clothes, and when they went out to fight wore great coats of mail. These men were great thieves, and stole all that came in their way.

Some of these men sailed from Den-mark in the year 900, and, in a storm, were cast on the shores of Ice-land. Thus Ice-land was found by chance, and in a few years some Danes went there to live, and kept up a trade with the main-land. When some years had gone by, Green-land was found by an Ice-land-er who set sail in a way that no one else had gone, and in a short time some of the Ice-land folks went to live in the new land where there was less ice and snow.

You would think from the name that it was a place where green grass grew, and there were green fields, and green trees, and high green hills such as you can see in your own land. But if you look on the map you will see that this could not be; for Green-land is near the North Pole, where there is ice and snow all the year round, and the folks there have to live in huts, that have a hole in the side for them to crawl through, and a hole in the top to let the smoke out.

Eric, the Red, was one of the first who went from Ice-land to Green-land to make a home. Men in those days were as fond of change as they are now, and as they had but few clothes and did not need much to keep house with, they could go from place to place with great ease.

Their ships were strange in shape, with a tall prow in front, and must have been made stout and strong or they could not have stood the rough waves in the great north sea. How would you like to live where there were ice and snow all the time, and the sun did not shine bright or warm for six months at a time.

I have said that the Danes kept up a trade with the main-land; but it was not the land that you will see near Green-land or Ice-land on the map. They did not know that such a great land was so near; for when they set sail they took but one course and that was to the land they had come from, which was Den-mark.

You can judge by the map how far off that was, and will not think it strange that it took so long a time to find out the great land that lay so near, but in a way they were not wont to go.

One of the men who went with Eric, the Red, had a son, who at that time was in Nor-way, with which a trade was kept up. When the son came back to Ice-land and found that those with whom he made his home were not there, he made up his mind to go to Green-land too, though he did not know how to get there, and there was no one to show him the way.

But for all that he set out with a ship's crew, and might have found his way to Green-land, if a storm had not set in that drove him out of his course. Part of the time they were shut in by thick fogs, so that they could not tell where they were. Then the bleak winds blew from the north and drove their ship far to the south-west, when their aim had been to keep to the north-east.

At length they saw a land which they knew could not be Green-land, for they had been told that its shores were rough and full of ice-hills, and these shores were quite flat and great trees grew there; so they stood out to sea, and in two days with a south-west wind they came in sight of a coast, which was also flat and full of trees. This did not please them, so they set sail once more and in three days came to a third land, which they found out had the sea on all sides and was not as large as Ice-land. Its great ice-hills they did not like, so they did not land, but bore off with the same wind, and in four days came to the coast of Green-land. This was in the year 986. If they had known that the land they had been so near was part of a great and a new world, how changed would have been their course! But the men were sick of the sea and glad to get back to their own homes and their friends, and to tell them all they had seen.

In eight years this same man, whose name was Bard-son, and who had a ship of his own, went off to spend some time with the Earl of Nor-way to whom he spoke of the strange land he had seen but a few days' sail from Green-land; and the Earl, and all those who heard him, thought it was a great shame that he did not go on shore when he was so near, and had such a good chance to find out what sort of a place it was.

The young men of Green-land were quite sure they would not have done as Bard-son did; and as they had no books to read, and not much else to think of, their whole talk for years and years was of what some of their own folks had seen with their own eyes. It was so strange a tale that some of them did not think it could be true.

Green trees and a flat coast so near? It could not be! The men had dreamt it! No one cared to send a ship down that way to see if it were so. They did not care a great deal for land. The great sea was the field they plow'd; it gave them their food, and they could ride at ease on its waves and feel free to go here or there.

But in the year 1,000, Leif, one of the sons of Eric, the Red, made up his mind to go out in search of those strange lands of which he had heard since he was a boy, and to find out if these tales were all true. So he bought the same ship that Bard-son used to call his own, the name of which has not come down to us, and with quite a large crew set sail from *Green-land.*

The first land they made was that which Bard-son had seen last. Here they went on shore. Not a blade of grass was to be seen; on all sides were great hills of ice, and twixt these and the shore a great bare field of slate, on which no weed could find a place to grow. As they did not like the looks of the land they gave it a bad name, Hell-u-land, and put to sea at once.

It is thought that this land was what is now known as New-found-land, which sets out from the main-land so that the waves can dash all round its coast, and the north winds pile their drifts of ice and snow up on the shore.

The next land these brave men came to, and where they went on shore, was quite flat, but thick woods could be seen back from the low coast. To this place they gave the name of Wood-land. It is now known as No-va Sco-tia.

But Leif did not choose to stay here; so he set sail, and in a few days came to a point of land that set out at the east of the main-land like a great bare arm of stone, or a hook to reap with. This you will see, if you look on the map, was Cape Cod, and through Cape Cod Bay, Leif went with his ship and soon found a nice place to land on the coast of Mas-sa-chu-setts. Here they at first built huts to live in; but as they liked the place and made up their minds to stay for some time, they put up log houses in which they could keep warm when the days grew cold, and ice and snow were on the ground.

From time to time men were sent out to view the land, and one day when one of them, a German, did not come back with the rest, Leif and a few of his crew went out to look for him. They soon met him, and he told them he had not been far, but had found vines and grapes which were well known to him, as he had been born in a land where they grew. At first they did not think he told the truth; but the next day some of the men went with him, and found it just as he had said it was.

When Leif and his men made up their minds to go home, they piled the deck of their ship with the trees they had cut down, and filled the long boat with grapes. The place was so full of vines and grapes that Leif gave it the name of Vin-land; and in the spring he and his men set out for Green-land.

These brave Norse men and their sons could not tell the rest of the world what they had seen; so years went by and few found their way to this new world. Now and then a ship went out from Ice-land or Green-land, and there is proof that these North men found their way down the coast of North A-mer-i-ca as far as Mas-sa-chu-setts and Rhode Is-land.

Bronze breast-plates, bronze belts, and sword-hilts, have been found from time to time, which could not have been worn by the red men of the woods, who had no use for such things. Strange signs were found cut in the rocks, and at New-port there is now a round house of gray stone which was built, no one knows when, but long ere Co-lum-bus came to A-mer-i-ca.

At this time, and for a long term of years, the whole of the U-ni-ted States, from the At-lan-tic to the Mis-sis-sip-pi, was a wild land where great woods grew, and where bears, wolves, wild-cats, and deer were free to roam. Here and there at the foot of high hills were wide fields of long grass that spread for miles and miles like a great green sea. Snakes of all kinds made their home in this long grass through which they slid with ease, and basked in the warm rays of the sun. Here, too, the wild ox made a path, and went back and forth where the foot of man had not trod, and no one had as yet found out the worth of his horns and his skin.

It is said that long ere a white man saw this land, strange men with dark skins lived here and built large towns, fought great fights, and served false gods. But of this we can not be sure. No one can tell what took place, or what they did who lived here in those far off days when no white man had set foot on the land.

The first white men who came to this new world found here a wild race who wore the skins of wild beasts tied round their waists, and lived in a rude sort of way. They were tall and straight, with dark red skins, high cheek bones, and coarse black hair. The whites gave these red men the name of In-di-ans, as it was then thought that A-mer-i-ca was a part of In-di-a.

These In-di-ans could do three things: hunt, fish, and fight. They made their squaws do all the hard work. These poor squaws had to dig the ground, sow the corn, and weave the mats of which their huts were made; and not a smile or a kind word did they get to pay them for their hard tasks.

The men spent the most of their time in the woods, where they could hunt for game, by the streams where fish were to be caught, or else in fights with those who dwelt near them.

They made use of bows and clubs with great skill. Their darts had sharp stones at the end, or bits of shells. They were such good shots that they could bring down a bird, or a deer, or a man a long way off. Their clubs were made of hard wood. When they killed a man, they would cut off his scalp, which was the skin of his head with the hair on, and these scalps were tied to their belts and worn with much pride.

These were not nice men to meet with in a strange land, and as you read on you will learn how the white men had to fight these foes, and in what ways they tried to make friends with the red men.

CHAPTER II.

A GREAT MAN.

At the time of which I write, the earth was thought to be flat, and men who went to sea made use of the stars to steer by.

But a great change came, and a great man. His name was Chris-to-pher Co-lum-bus, and he was born at Gen-o-a, It-a-ly. As a boy he was fond of the sea, and he learned, while quite a lad, how to sail a ship and to take charge of a crew. When he grew to be a man he had a ship of his own, and kept up a trade with lands that were far off. In those days men went to Af-ri-ca for gold and for slaves, and to A-sia for rich fruits and fine goods that could be found no where else. The sea was a great high-way, and bad men would lie in wait to seize the ships on their way back from the East, and to take from each one of them the rich prize that it bore.

Of course the men did not want to lose what they had gone so far to get, and there would be great fights on the sea.

In a sea-fight off the coast of Spain Co-lum-bus' ship was set on fire, and all on board had to swim for their lives. Co-lum-bus found his way to Lis-bon, where there were some folks who spoke his tongue, and they gave him the best of care. Here he made his home, and took a wife, and in time had charts and books of his own, that told him all that was known of the great wide sea, of which he was so fond.

Each day he grew more wise, and his mind was full of great schemes.

From what he read, and from what he had seen in his trips to far off coasts, from the shape of the land and the bend of the sky, Co-lum-bus made up his mind that the world was round and not so large as it was thought to be, and that men must sail west to find a short way to In-di-a.

If you look at a map of the world you will see that the short cut from Eu-rope to In-di-a would be straight through North A-mer-i-ca. No ship could make this, of course. But at the time I speak of, the folks in Eu-rope did not know that there was such a place as North A-mer-i-ca, and Co-lum-bus thought it would be a fine thing to take this short cut from Spain to In-di-a. The more he thought of it, the more he felt that it could be done. He was both brave and bold. He did not ask that men and ships should be sent to see if this were so. He wished to take the lead and to prove that he was not such a fool as they thought.

What faith he had!

For long, long years he tried hard to prove that this thing could be done;

but no one had faith in him. They had been taught that the earth was flat, and that it was not safe for ships to go west for fear they would fall off.

He could get no help in his plans, and wise men told him to give them up. He asked in vain for ships and gold, for he was too poor to buy what he would need on such a long trip. Some made fun of him to his face and said, if the world were round, some folks would have to walk on their heads.

One day when Co-lum-bus felt worn and sad, for it was a great grief to him that he could get no one to think as he did, he sat down to rest in the shade of a house where some monks made their home.

It was high noon, and he asked the monk to give him a cool drink. The monk brought him the draught, and sat down by Co-lum-bus to have a talk with him. Co-lum-bus told him his views and his plans, and the monk thought so well of them that he said he would speak to his friends at the court of Spain and see what they would do to aid him in his bold scheme.

Co-lum-bus first went to It-a-ly, in 1484, but the king of that place would give him no help. Then he went to Por-tu-gal, and bad men laid a scheme to fit him out with ships and then rob him of the wealth or fame he might win. But Co-lum-bus found this out, and when the king of Por-tu-gal sought to make terms with him, Co-lum-bus would give him no heed.

This will show you how he came to go to Spain and to sail from there, when he was born in Gen-o-a, and had made his home in Lis-bon for so many years.

In the mean time he had sent a friend to Eng-land, to see what King Hen-ry the Sev-enth would do for him. This friend fell in with those sea thieves I have told you of, and they took all that he had, so that when he got to Eng-land he was in a sad plight. He was sick for some time, but as soon as he got well he went to work and made and sold maps, and in a year or two he had the means to buy clothes that were fit to wear at court. And not till then did he go to see the king. This was in the year 1488.

Co-lum-bus had gone to Spain to try his luck there, and found a friend in good Queen Is-a-bel-la. He had made up his mind to go to France if Spain would not fit him out with ships; and if it had not been for the queen, Co-lum-bus might have died and the New World might not have been found at all. But these things do not take place by chance.

When the right time comes, God puts it in the hearts of men to do what is wise and good in His sight. And God put it in the heart of Queen Is-a-bel-la to help Co-lum-bus just at this time. "All things work for good to them that love God."

The monk who had been so kind to Co-lum-bus and such a friend to the cause from the first, set out to see what the king and queen of Spain would do. They were in camp at San-ta Fe, where the court was held, with the troops who at that time laid siege to Gra-na-da. The Fra, as the monk was called, told them that he had great faith in Co-lum-bus, who was a wise and good man, and there was no doubt that he had the skill to do all that he laid out. To such a man there was no such word as fail.

The Fra said it would be a great loss if they let slip so fair a chance to add to the wealth of Spain, and it would not do to let Co-lum-bus go off in a rage, and have the rich prize fall in the hands of kings who would be glad to seize it from the grasp of Spain.

So well did he plead that the queen bade that Co-lum-bus should be sent for, with gold from the king's purse to pay his way. Co-lum-bus came and spoke in strong terms; some thought what he said was wise, and were pleased with the way he spoke; some thought him a vain man, and his terms much too high. The war had cost Spain a great deal of gold, and they had none to waste on such a wild scheme as this in which Co-lum-bus would like them to take part.

Co-lum-bus gave up all hopes. Hymns were sung, and feasts were spread, and all Spain was glad, for Gra-na-da had been won from the hands of the foe. No one had time to think of poor Co-lum-bus, who felt that the years he had spent in Spain were in truth lost years. He took leave of his friends and set out for Cor-do-va, from which port he could sail for France where, as I have told you, he thought he might find friends to aid him in his plans. This was in the first month of the year 1492.

At this time, one of the men who served the crown and had great love and zeal for the land that gave him birth, went to the queen and spoke to her as none but a man of his rank would dare to speak. He said that it was a shame that so grand a scheme should fall through for want of some one like the queen to give it aid. She was fond of good deeds, and glad to do all she could to build up the church of Christ, and raise the Cross in lands where His name was not known. It was a sin to lose such a chance to let the light in a dark place. Why should they let a small sum of gold stand in the way of such a grand work and such a great prize?

If Co-lum-bus would risk his life, could Spain not risk her gold? Friends and foes of his dear land would blame those who had been so blind and so weak as not to seize on this chance, and in the years to come each child of Spain would feel the loss and shame of it.

The queen could not be deaf to these words. She said she would pledge her own gems to get the means, if Spain could not spare the gold. But there was no need of this.

A man was sent in great haste to Co-lum-bus whom he found on the bridge of Pi-nas, two miles from Gra-na-da, and when he came back to the town of San-ta-Fe, he found the folks there so kind and good that he gave no thought to the things that had vexed him.

Those whom God means shall do great things have to fight their way through much that is hard and sad. This makes them brave and strong, if they are made of the right kind of stuff.

What joy must have been in the heart of Co-lum-bus when he was told that the king and queen of Spain would fit out a fleet of ships, and place him at the head!

At a sea port of Spain, named Pa-los, three small craft were put in charge of Co-lum-bus. They were such poor ships that he had hard work to find men to go in them as crews. Few men in our day would care to risk their lives in such poor ships as the king and queen of Spain gave to Co-lum-bus. But it was the best they could do. The king said the crews must go on board and do as Co-lum-bus said, and they went, but in great fear, for they shrank from such a wild cruise and were sure they would not find their way back to their homes.

The three ships were named the San-ta Ma-ri-a [Ma-ree-ah] the Pin-ta, and the Ni-na [Ne-nah.] Co-lum-bus went on board the San-ta Ma-ri-a which had a deck. The Pin-ta and the Ni-na had no decks, and there was deep gloom in Pa-los when the fleet put out to sea in 1492. At the end of a week they were out of sight of land. Great fear fell on the crews, who had no wish but to get back home as fast as they could. The wind blew them on in a straight course, and this made them fear that they should not have a fair wind to take them back.

The sea gulls, and the weeds, and the small birds they met at break of day made them think the land was near, and when the sun rose and they saw but the broad, deep sea, they were wroth with the man who had brought them so far from home. Their hopes gave way to fears as day by day they watched and saw no signs of land. They had been made to go on this wild cruise. Their hearts were not in it. They had left all that was dear to them, and for what?

Some of the rough men shed tears, and some gave vent to loud cries. All of them found fault with Co-lum-bus, and thought he was to blame for all their woes. He had led them off in search of a land that was no-where to be found, and they had a mind to kill him if he did not turn back. Then they would soon change the ship's course, and when they got back to Spain would tell the king that Co-lum-bus fell in the sea while his gaze was fixed on the stars. Co-lum-bus stood firm. He tried to soothe the men, and to lift up their hearts. He told them of the wealth in store for them in the new land he was quite sure he should find, and which could not be far off, and in this way and by the threats that he made kept the men from crime. He said that he was bound by the help of God to go to In-di-a, and if they did not do as they ought it would be worse for *them when the word was sent to the king of Spain.

In a few days the wind blew from the right course, the sea was calm, and the three ships stood so near that Co-lum-bus could talk to those in charge of the Pin-ta and Ni-na. The air had a sweet smell, and fields of sea-weed came near the ship. While Co-lumbus bent his head on the chart to see if he could have gone out of his track, a shout went up from the Pin-ta, and the cry of " Land! Land!"

The men were wild with joy. Co-lum-bus knelt down and gave thanks to God. The crews on all of the ships joined in a song of praise. Some of the men climb to the mast head, and strain their eyes to see the land that lay but a few leagues off. All that night, to please the men who were so sure it was the land, Co-lum-bus set the ship out of its course, and stood to the north west. The light of day put an end to all their hopes, as to a dream. What they had thought was land was but a dark cloud! With hearts full of grief they once more turn their course to the west, and for some days sail on with the same fair wind, smooth sea, and bright skies.

The one who first saw the land was to have a great prize, and this kept the men on the watch. But if one should cry out Land! and it did not prove to be so, he was to have no share in the prize, though his eyes might be the first to catch a glimpse of the real land, and his voice the first to tell the good news. Once those on board the Ni-na, which took the lead the most of the time, fired a gun, and sent up a flag and were sure they had seen land; but as they went on they found out that they were wrong.

All this time the crew of the San-ta Ma-ri-a had it in their hearts to kill Co-lum-bus, and he knew it, but showed no fear, though he kept a close watch on all the signs that told him the land could not be far off.

They had been at least two months at sea, a long

time for men of ill-will to keep their rage in check, when birds and land fowl that Co-lum-bus knew could not fly far, came quite near the ship. The songs of birds were in the air, and one day the men on board the Pin-ta took up a staff on which strange signs were wrought, and saw a cane float by, and a large lot of weeds torn fresh from the shore.

Co-lum-bus spoke to his men; told them how good God had been to them to lead them so far and keep them safe from all harm, and said that as he had sure proofs they were near land he would have them watch all night.

New joy rose in the hearts of the home-sick men. Not an eye was closed that night. The breeze had been fresh all day with more sea than they had had for some time, and the ships went with more speed. As it grew dark Co-lum-bus took his stand on the top of the high deck of his ship, and kept his eyes fixed on the west.

At ten o'clock at night he thought he saw a light on shore. It came and went, as if it were a torch in a boat that rose and sunk with the waves, or in the hand of some one on shore borne up and down as he went from house to house. In two hours more the shout of Land! Land! was heard from the Pin-ta, and the ships laid to, to wait for the dawn.

What pride and joy

must have been in the heart of Co-lum-bus! Those who had thought him a fool would now learn that he was a wise man.

At break of day they saw a long strip of low land five miles to the north. Trees rise in view and the shores are green. All shed tears of joy, and sing a hymn of praise to God.

The crews man the boats and in great pomp row to the shore. Co-lum-bus lands in a rich dress, and with a drawn sword in his hand. The flag of Spain is set up which has on it a green cross with crowns and the names of Fer-di-nand and Is-a-bel-la. All kneel on the sand, and kiss the earth, and thank God with tears of joy. In this way Co-lum-bus lays claim to the land in the name of the king and queen of Spain, and all the men vow to serve Co-lum-bus, and through him the king and queen of the land they love.

CHAPTER III.

A NEW WORLD.

Co-lum-bus gave the name of San Sal-va-dor to this land which he thought was on the coast of In-di-a. He did not see the gold and gems he knew were to be found in that rich land, but he saw a new race of men with dark skins, who wore no clothes at all, and stared at him and his men as if they thought they had come down from the sky, or out of the deep sea. When these red men on the land saw the boats draw near the shore, and a lot of strange men clad in bright steel and gay clothes land on the beach, they fled to the woods in great fear.

But when they found that no one sought to harm them they came back and drew near the men of Spain with great awe, fell on their knees, and made signs as if they thought they were gods.

These men were not so dark as Af-ri-cans, nor was their hair so crisp. It was straight and coarse, cut short at the tops of the ears, and some locks left long hung down their backs. Each man held a long lance in his hand the point of which was made hard by fire, while some of them were made more sharp by a piece of flint, or the teeth or bone of a fish. They knew not the use of a sword, and when one was held out to them they took it by the edge.

Co-lum-bus gave them gay caps, glass beads, hawks' bells, and such things as were used in trade on the gold coast of Af-ri-ca, and made friends of them at once. They hung the beads round their necks, and were pleased with their fine toys, and with the sound of the bells.

When Co-lum-bus asked these men, to whom he gave the name of In-di-ans, where he could find gold, they would point to the south, and make signs that led him to think that a king dwelt there of such wealth that his food was served on plates of wrought gold. He heard, too, some talk of Cu-ba, and of large ships that went there to trade, and he made up his mind that all these bits of land he saw were on the coast of A-si-a, and that the ships were those of the Great Khan, of whom he had read.

So he set sail for Cu-ba, where he thought to find mines of gold, groves of spice, and shores full of pearls, but when he got there he found no signs of wealth. One man of the tribe who came out to meet him wore a ring—and that was in his nose! But though the land was not rich in gold it was rich in much else that would bring wealth to those who set up a trade with these new lands, which are now known as the West In-dies.

As Co-lum-bus steered his boat by the east coast of Cu-ba he saw land to the south-east, with great high hills that rose up to the sky. The In-di-ans cried out in a way that made Co-lum-bus think that that was the place to look for gold, but when they saw him steer his boat that way they were in great fear and made signs to him to come back. They told him as well as they could that a fierce race dwelt there, that they had but one eye, and would eat a man up raw.

But Co-lum-bus went on and in two days came to a fine piece of land to which he gave the name of Hay-ti [Ha-tee]. High rocks rose from out a rich growth of trees, the soil was rich, broad plains of green grass lay at the foot of the hills; and the fires at night and the smoke that was seen by day, were signs that more men would be found here than they had seen else where in the New World. But though the soil was rich, the streams full of fish, and the In-di-ans kind, the men of Spain were sad, for they saw no signs of gold.

Co-lum-bus found at Hay-ti, now known as San Do-min-go, a race of men not at all like those he had met with. Some of them wore rings and chains of gold, which they were glad to change for the beads and bells the crews gave them. A young chief came to see Co-lum-bus and gave him a rich belt and two bits of gold; and he and all his men thought that

THE PILGRIMS FIGHTING THE INDIANS

Co-lum-bus and those with him must have come down from the skies.

Though not much gold was found in this place, Co-lum-bus was told by one of the wise men that he would soon reach the lands that were rich in this ore. It was near the end of the year 1492, when Co-lum-bus and his crews came to the Bay of Saint Thom-as. Some of the men on shore came off in boats made of light bark; some swam to them and all brought gifts of rare fruits, and with free hands gave all the gold they wore.

The chief who ruled the land sent to Co-lum-bus a broad belt wrought with gay beads and bones, and a mask of wood, the eyes, nose, and tongue of which were of gold. The chief sent word that it was his wish that the ships should come to that part of the coast near which he dwelt.

As the wind was not right, Co-lum-bus could not get his boats off at once, so he sent one of his head men who was well read in the law, with some of the crew to call on the chief, whom they found in a large and well-built town which was called Pun-ta San-ta. The chief met the men in a kind of square, which had been swept clean and made fine, and did all he could to show how glad he was to see them. When they left he gave them birds and bits of gold, and crowds of men went with them to their boats.

When Co-lum-bus set sail

out of this bay, the wind was from the land, and so light that it did not fill the sails. It was Christ-mas eve. Co-lum-bus had kept watch each night since they left Spain. This night as the sea was calm and smooth, and the ship scarce moved at all, he thought he would lie down and rest. He felt quite safe as the boats that were out that day found no rocks nor shoals in their course.

As soon as Co-lum-bus left the deck the man whose place it was to steer the San-ta Ma-ri-a gave the helm in charge of one of the ship-boys, and went to sleep. The rest of the men who had the watch, now that Co-lum-bus was out of the way, thought that they might as well take their ease, and in a short time the whole crew had gone to sleep. In the mean time the strong tides that ran by this coast swept the ship with no noise but with great force up on a sand bank. The boy could not have been a smart lad, for it is said that he took no heed of the big waves whose loud roar could be heard for at least three miles. But as soon as he felt the boat strike and heard the wild rush of the sea, he gave a loud cry for help. Co-lum-bus was the first on deck. He and his men did their best to save the ship, but it was too late. The keel was fixed deep in the sand, and as the sea would soon break her up, Co-lum-bus and his crew went on board the Ni-na.

It is not well to set a boy to do a man's work. Co-lum-bus knew this, and was not to blame for the loss of the ship. The wreck took place on the shore near where the chief dwelt, and he went on board the Ni-na to see Co-lum-bus, and wept to find him so much cast down.

While the two stood on deck they saw a light bark draw near in which were some In-di-ans who had brought a lot of bright bits of gold, which they wished to change for hawks' bells. These toys gave the In-di-ans great joy. I will tell you why. The In-di-ans were fond of the dance, and would mark the time with the strange songs they sung, and take their steps to the sound of a kind of drum, made from the trunk of a tree, and the noise that could be made with small bits of wood. When they hung the hawks' bells on their necks, waists, and arms, and heard the clear sweet sound they gave, in time with each move that was made in the dance, the In-di-ans were wild with joy. It is said that one In-di-an gave half a hand-full of gold-dust for one of these bells, and fled to the woods for fear the men of Spain would rob him when they found out how cheap they had sold it.

When the chief saw how the face of Co-lum-bus lit up at the sight of the gold, and found out that it was his wish to reach a land where this ore could be dug out of the ground, he told him by signs that there was a place not far off where there was so much gold that the folks there did not care much for it.

This news brought good cheer to the heart of Co-lum-bus and he felt that his ship-wreck was not such a sad thing as he had thought. But for fear the Pin-ta or the Ni-na should meet with the same fate as the San-ta Ma-ri-a, he thought it best to go back to Spain and make it known what a great and a rich land he had found.

On his way back there rose a great storm. Co-lum-bus thought his ships would go down and the good news be lost to Spain. So he wrote it all out, sealed it up in a cake of wax, put the wax in a cask, and threw the cask in the sea.

But God took care of the brave men, and his crews, and the ships found their way to port. When Co-lum-bus told of all the strange sights he had seen, there was great joy in Spain. Some of his men had brought back with them great lumps of gold; and when they showed these to their friends, all had a strong wish to go to the New World and get rich at once.

Large fleets of ships set sail from Spain, Port-u-gal, and It-a-ly. Some of them found the same lands that Co-lum-bus had seen, and some of them found their way to the main-land.

There were some folks who thought it was no

great thing that Co-lum-bus had done. It is told that at a feast a fine young man in a court dress said that he did not think it was hard to find such a land.

Co-lum-bus bade him make an egg stand on end. He tried and could not do it. Then Co-lum-bus broke the end of the egg so that it stood with ease, and in this way taught the vain man that he knew less than he thought he did.

Co-lum-bus went three or four times to the West In-di-es, and on each trip he took hosts of men to join him in the search for gold. But they had hard work to live in the strange lands, and they did not pick up the gold they thought they should find in all the fields. This did not please them at all, and they grew cross, and thought Co-lum-bus was to blame for all they had to put up with.

The fourth time Co-lum-bus crossed the sea he found land at a point south of the West In-di-es, and this was the first that was known of the large tract of land which we call South A-mer-i-ca. This was in 1498.

The fame of Co-lum-bus won for him the hate of great men at the court of Spain, and they did all they could to harm him. False tales were told; and men he had thought were his friends, and for whom he had done so much, did not treat him well, and he was sent back to Spain in chains. Was it not hard to drive him out of the New World that might not have been found at all but for him? What poor pay he got for all he had gone through!

It was still worse for Co-lum-bus when Queen Is-a-bel-la died, for then he had no kind friend at court to save him from the wrath of his foes. No one took pains to see that he had food to eat or clothes to wear, and so he had to do the best that he could. He died at last, a poor lone old man, who did not know how much good he had done in the world, nor dream of the great fame that would be his for all time to come.

In the year 1512, an old man, whose name was Ponce de Le-on, set sail from Spain to seek for a fount of which he had heard. If he could bathe in it he would be young and gay once more. His search was vain. But he found a part of the New World which had not yet been seen by men from the old, and he gave it the name of Flo-ri-da.

In one of the ships that set sail from It-a-ly was a man named A-mer-i-cus Ves-pu-ci-us, and he went all round the coast of South A-mer-i-ca where no one else had been. When he went back home he wrote of all he had seen, and said that he had been the first to find the main land, and so they gave the name of A-mer-i-ca to the New World to which Co-lum-bus had first led the way.

The king of Eng-land heard what had been done by Spain, and he sent men and ships to the New World. Some of them had the bad luck to land in the cold north, in the midst of ice and snow. Some found their way south, where the air was soft and mild, and birds sang, and the fields were green the whole year round.

Men came from all parts to seek homes in the New World, and to grow rich on the gold that was there. They had to work hard to till the soil, to cut down trees, and to fight their way through the dense swamps and thick woods. Some died for want of food. For some the life was too hard. But those that were left were brave and strong, and kept right on in their work, and from time to time fresh crews came from the Old World to give them cheer.

A man, named John Cab-ot, as soon as he heard of what Co-lum-bus had done, set sail from Eng-land, by the King's leave, and made his way to the New World. He went too far to the north where he found the land so bleak and so cold that he did not care to stay, and soon made his way back to the place he came from.

In a short time his son Se-bas-tian set sail with as large a crew as he could hire, and kept his ship well to the west. At length he came in sight of land. But there were no green fields, no ripe fruits, nor birds, such as Co-lum-bus and his men had seen. As far as the eye could see there were bleak rocks, dark pine trees, and heaps of snow. White bears made their homes in deep caves, and the woods were full of a strange kind of deer. This was not the place to look for gold, and Se-bas-tian went back to Eng-land with a sad heart.

All this time men from Spain and the lands near by, went to the south part of the New World where they found gold and things of great worth. They were for the most part bad men who thought they had a right to kill the In-di-ans and steal their land. Some times the men of Spain had a great fight with the red men, and drove them out of the land. This was what Cor-tes did in Mex-i-co. Some times the red men had the best of the fight, and shot at the white men and drove them back to their ships.

Then the French thought they must have a share in the New World, so they sent men and ships to the west. Some of them went as far north as the Gulf of Saint Law-rence, and up to the place where Mon-tre-al now stands. The In-di-ans here were much scared at first at the sight of white men. But in a short time they grew used to them, and brought the French men food, and herbs to cure those who were sick, and were as kind as they knew how to be. How did the French men pay them for the use they made of them as guides through these strange, wild lands? I will tell you. They caught the In-di-an chief and took him by force to France. The King of France thought there was no harm in this, and so he sent this base man, Car-tier, back to the New World, and with him one who was to act as a sort of king in the land which Car-tier had seen, and to which he had no more right than you or I. But this time the In-di-ans would have nought to do with the white men. They did not hurt the French men, but they would give them no food and would not act as guides. This served them just right. Some grew sick; some died; and the rest went back to France, and made up their minds that the New World was not a fit place for a white man to live in.

But the King of France had no mind to let the King of Spain have more than his share of the New World. So he sent more men and more ships, and one of these men went by the coast of Flo-ri-da, and all the way up to New-found-land, and set up the flag of the French king, and gave the place the name of New France. This was in the year 1524.

Do you know how much a score is? It is twice ten. If one score is twice ten, then four score must be eight times ten. Well, I have told you that when

Se-bas-tian Cab-ot went back to Eng-land he said that A-mer-i-ca was a poor cold place, where bears and deer lived, and no gold could be found. So for four score years Eng-land sent no ships to the New World.

At length a bold young man, named Wal-ter Ra-leigh (raw-lee), made up his mind to go and see if what Cab-ot said was true. Queen E-liz-a-beth, who ruled Eng-land at that time, was fond of Ra-leigh, and she gave him leave to seize the new lands he might find and lay claim to them in her name. All he had to do was to set up the flag of Great Brit-ain, and draw his sword from its sheath. His ships steered to the south west, and came to a land where there was no ice or snow, and green trees and ripe grapes grew close to the shore. The In-di-ans came down to meet the white men, and gave them corn, or maize. as they called it, and fish. Ra-leigh gave to the new land he found the name of Vir-gin-ia, and he left men at Ro-an-oake, where he first went on shore, and spent much gold in the hope that a large town would be built there and be called by his name. But ere this could be done Spain found out that the Eng-lish flag had been set up on the coast, and went to work to drive off the ships that were sent down. Ra-leigh did not lose heart. But at this time news came that the King of Spain with a large fleet of ships of war was on its way to lay siege to Eng-land, and so Eng-land had need of all her ships, and Ra-leigh's with the rest. So the poor folks on the coast of Vir-gin-ia were left to starve and die.

Though Eng-land and France laid claim to a large part of North A-mer-i-ca, it was a long, long time ere they sent men to make homes in the New World, to clear off the wild lands, and to till the soil and plant such things as would grow there.

CHAPTER IV.

NEW HOMES.

In the year 1606, the King of Eng-land, whose name was James the First, gave a large tract of land in Vir-gin-ia to some men who had found out it was a fine place for poor men, as the streams were full of fish, and the woods were full of game. Ship loads of folks with small means, set sail from Eng-land, and made their homes at a place they called James-town.

The red men came to see them and to smoke their pipe of peace with the white men, and for a while all went well. But as soon as they found that the white men had come to rob them of their lands, and to drive them from the soil to which they felt they had the first and best right they grew cold and stern, and were friends no more.

They were a strange race and their mode of life was not at all like ours. The red men had no books. They could hunt and fish, and raise corn and beans and such things; and with rude skill made their bows and darts, and the bowls in which to pound their corn. Their boats were made of birch-bark, and their huts, of bark or mats, were in the shape of a cone. They were fond of war, and proud of the scalps they won from their foes. They had no fear of death, and would scorn to plead for their lives.

The white men gave them guns and rum; and these two things were the cause of much strife, and made the red men hard to deal with.

With the band who came from Eng-land was one John Smith, who was wise and brave, and knew how to deal with the red men, and but for him the white men would soon have been swept out of Vir-gin-ia. He was taught how to fight when a boy, and had been in great wars. He had led a wild life, and once, it is said, he fought with three Turks, cut off their heads and bore them to his tent. He was young and strong, and so wise and good that the white men made him their chief. He did not like to hear an oath, and he made a law that each man who swore was to have a cold bath and sleep in his wet clothes. This soon put a stop to that sin of the tongue.

Some of the white men were not fond of good John Smith. They thought he knew too much and held his head too high, and they laid a plot to drive him out of Vir-gin-ia. They had come to seek gold and did not want to work, and did not plant crops as they should have done. So, of course, there was lack of food. This made them ill, and the loss by death was so great, that the rest of the band made up their minds to leave the place.

But John Smith did not lose heart. He spoke to the men in words of cheer, and would not let them launch their boats. While some of the men spent their time in a vain search for gold, he was on the look out for food for them to eat. While they wept and sighed for home, he built huts, took care of the sick, and kept on good terms with the red men.

One day John Smith set out on foot with a few men to see more of the new land. They fell in the hands of a fierce band of red men who put all but John Smith to death. He was quite calm, and when they saw him write and do strange things, they were in great fear of him. For a while they kept him as a show; then they said he must die.

Smith was bound hand and foot and laid on the ground. His head was on a great stone. The big club was raised to dash out his brains when a child ten or twelve years of age sprang from the crowd, put her arms round the poor man's neck and plead for his life. Her name was Po-ca-hon-tas, and she was the dear child of the great chief Pow-hat-an. She was fond of John Smith, and could not bear to see him killed; so for her sake he was set free.

This young girl twice saved the life of John Smith at the risk of her own, and she is said to have been as fond of him as if she were his own child.

In the same year that this took place, that is in 1608, a small band of men tried to fly from Eng-land with their wives and young folks. As they drew near the sea shore a great crowd gave chase, and they were seized and shut up in jail.

What had they done? They were poor, but that was no crime. They loved God, and tried to do what was right. They were fond of the word of God, and read in it a great deal, and each night and morn they prayed that God would bless them and teach them His will. This did not please the king, who said there must be but one church, and those who loved God must serve him in one way.

The more these poor men

read the word of God the more they felt that the king's way was not the right way. So they made up their minds not to go to the king's church; and those who were too poor to build a church to suit their own taste met in their own homes, or in barns, or in fields, and prayed and sang psalms their own way.

This put the king in a great rage, and he set men to work to do all they could to vex these Pu-ri-tans. They left them no peace, and those who could not stand the fight went back to the king's church. Those who would not yield to threats or force sought to leave their homes and find a safe place in the New World. But the king would not let them go or stay at home in peace, and so when they tried to leave Eng-land they were caught like thieves and shut up in jail.

The next spring the Pu-ri-tans were more wise. They laid their plans in such a way that not a word got to the king's ears, and they made out to set sail from Eng-land. They went to Hol-land, where they dwelt for some years. But in course of time they grew sad when they thought of home. They were in a strange land. The folks there spoke a strange tongue. They did not dare to go back to Eng-land, for fear King James would treat them worse than he had done, so they thought it best to go to A-mer-i-ca where they could pray as they chose, and still be with the old flag and serve Eng-land.

It was in the fall of the year 1620 when five score Pu-ri-tans set sail from the port of Ply-mouth in the ship May Flow-er, for New Eng-land, which was the name John Smith gave to all that part of A-mer-i-ca that lay north of Vir-gin-ia. For more than two months they were at sea. The winds and waves were rough, and one of their band died on the way. They came at last to Cape Cod, where they found a rough and rock bound coast. The spray froze on their clothes. There was not much to cheer them. It took them some time to find a place where they could build their homes.

At length a spot was found, where the soil seemed to be good, and* there were fine clear springs where they could quench their thirst. They called the place New Ply-mouth, and the stone on which they first set foot in the New World can be seen at this day. Weak and ill as the most of them were, they went to work to build a few huts in which they could live till the warm days came.

Day by day an old man, or a young wife, or a small child was borne out of the huts and a hole dug in the ground for a grave. But spring came; the birds sang in the woods; the sick folks found health in the air, and all was peace and joy.

When the Pil-grims who had made their homes in Ply-mouth wrote to their friends in Eng-land and told them how free they were, and that they could serve God as they chose, with no fear of the King or the head men of his church, those who were of the same mind in the Old World felt their hearts yearn for the shores of New Eng-land. The king was their foe. They were forced to meet and pray by stealth. Yet they knew that if they left Eng-land they would have to give up their nice homes, and to live in the woods, and put up with much that would be hard for them to bear. But they did not care so long as they were free, and could serve God in their own way.

At this time ships went each year from Eng-land to A-mer-i-ca, and men who went to trade, or to fish, had built huts on the coast. A man named Ma-son, who came from Hamp-shire, Eng-land, gave to a tract of land the name of New Hamp-shire. It is nice to know how the old towns and states got their names. Two small towns in New Hamp-shire, were known as Ports-mouth and Do-ver. 'Twixt these towns and New Ply-mouth the Pu-ri-tans made up their minds to make their new home. They first sent John En-di-cott with a few men to make the paths straight for their feet. He was a brave man with a kind heart, and was full of good cheer.

In the fall a ship came from Eng-land with more Pil-grims, but as she brought no stores of food, there was great fear that the whole band would starve to death. At one time they had but one pint of corn left, which was dealt out with great care, and each one of the band had five grains.

Yet, hard as was their lot, these brave men were full of faith, and hope, and trust in God. At the end of four years the Pu-ri-tans were in strong force in Mas - sa - chu - setts, where they built towns, and ships, and sowed large fields of corn and built mills to grind it.

One band made their way to a place which they called Bos-ton, as that was the name of the town in Eng-land from which the most of them had come. One band made their home on the coast, and gave to the place the name of Sa-lem.

CHAPTER V.

WARS WITH THE RED MEN.

At first the red men, or In-di-ans, were good friends with the whites, or Pu-ri-tans as they were now called; and brought them furs, and game, and fish, in change for hoes and cloth and such things. The whites were kind to them and they were kind to the whites. But this state of things did not last long. It made the red man's eye flash to see the white smoke curl up from the homes that were built on the ground where he and his brave men had been wont to meet and call their own. In the long cold nights as the red men sat round their camp fires they had hard thoughts of those who had laid out farms, and raised fine crops, and were so well off; and they laid plans to pounce on these homes of the white men some dark night, kill them in their beds, and seize their corn, their tools, and their warm clothes.

These bad thoughts took deep root in the hearts of the fierce tribe of Pe-quods who dwelt on the banks of a stream, now known as the Thames, on which, if you look on the map of Con-nec-ti-cut, you will see there is the town of New Lon-don.

A slight thing brought on the war, which broke out in 1637. The Pe-quods had a thirst for blood. The new homes were laid waste, no one felt safe. Fire and death met the white men in the fields, in their beds, in church or at home.

Some of the chiefs tried to get the Nar-ra-gan-sets to form a league, and kill all the white men in the land. The scheme came to the ears of Rog-er Wil-li-ams, and he set out with no one with him to see the head chief of the Nar-ra-gan-sets.

There he met the Pe-quod chiefs with the white man's blood still thick on their knives. They glared at Wil-li-ams, as if to tell him to look out for his scalp. But he had no fear of them. He sat down by his old friends Ca-non-i-cus and Mi-an-to-ni-mah, who had once saved his life in the woods, and was as calm as if he had been in his own house.

Three days and three nights he staid in the camp of the Nar-ra-gan-sets, and plead the cause of those who had sent him out of Bos-ton. Each night when he lay down to sleep he knew that he might be put to death by the Pe-quods. But his trust was in God, and he thought not of self.

On the fourth day the Nar-ra-gan-sets made up their minds that they would not join the Pe-quods. Rog-er Wil-li-ams went home with a glad heart, while the Pe-quod chiefs with fierce scowls slunk back to their tribe.

At the mouth of the Thames were the two chief forts of the Pe-quods, and these the men of Con-nect-ti-cut made up their minds lay low. They were but four score men and the Pe-quods were a large and fierce tribe. But the rage of the white men was great; their hearts were on fire. They had seen their friends killed and scalped, or borne to a fate worse than death, and day and night were in dread of a raid from these Pe-quods, whom they meant to show how white men could fight. Their plan was to sail down the coast past the mouth of the Thames, to land far up to the east and then march to the forts.

The Pe-quods saw them sail past, and at first did not know what to make of it. They made up their minds that the white men were scared, and set up loud shouts and songs that were heard at Ma-son's camp.

Long ere it was day on this May morn the dogs at the Pe-quod fort were heard to bark and howl. A cry went through the fort that the Eng-lish were at hand. As soon as it was light the white men sent their fire of shot at the red men's fort. The red men made good use of their bows and clubs; and as they were six to one at least, the fight was fierce and much blood was shed.

At last Ma-son cried out "We must burn them!" seized a fire-brand and thrust it in the dry mats of which the walls were made, and soon the whole fort was in a blaze. Choked and dazed by the smoke, the Pe-quods tried to fly, but Ma-son had ranged his troops on all sides, and when a red man showed his head he was shot down.

When the rest of the Pe-quods came down from their fort, and saw what the white men had done, they were in a great rage and made a rush at Ma-son to kill him. But a charge of shot from the white men's guns drove them back, and they fled to the woods. Troops came up from Mas-sa-chu-setts, and the Nar-ra-gan-set tribe lent their aid to the white men. The Pe-quods found no place of rest, for the white men kept close on their track, and in a short time there was not a Pe-quod to be found in all the land.

But you must not think that this brought to an end the wars with the red men. It takes a deep wound a long while to heal; and in the year 1675 a great war broke out, which is known as King Phil-ip's war.

It made King Phil-ip's heart swell with rage to see the white men drive back the In-di-ans and take their land as if the red men had no right to it. He laid a plot to get all the tribes to join, and fall on the white men and kill them. A red man ran in to one of the towns and told of this plot to the white men, and put them on their guard, and one night three of his tribe caught and killed him. These three In-di-ans were caught by some of the white men of Ply-mouth, tried by law, and hung for their crime. Phil-ip and his tribe could not bear this, and it brought on the war for which some think the whites were as much to blame as the reds.

Troops on horse and on foot went out of Bos-ton and Ply-mouth to aid the men in the small towns where King Phil-ip and his tribe had done much harm, and they kept close on the track of the red men.

King Phil-ip fled to a swamp to get out of the way of the troops. When the white men came to the swamp they saw no one, but they sent a shot each time they heard a noise or saw a bush shake, and in this way hurt some of their own friends. When night came on they formed a ring on the out side of the swamp, and made sure they would catch Phil-ip as soon as it was light. When the morn came he had gone with all his friends; no one knew where.

The next thing the white men heard was that the red-skins were at North-field and Deer-field. There was not a place in New Eng-land that was safe from the raids of the red men who had set out to kill the whites and to burn down their homes.

In the dead of night when all was still the fierce war-whoop of the red-skins would ring out from the woods. Soon a gleam of flame would burst from some house they had set on fire; then with yells and shouts the wild crew would leap in on those whom they had brought, with a start out of their sleep, and scalp them in their beds.

Some times when a white man went to the door of his house, and saw no foe in sight, a shot from an In-di-an hid by a tree would lay him low. Or he would leave his house to go to the field, hear a scream at his back, and find his wife and babes dead on the floor.

No one could feel safe.

To add to the fears of the white men, strange sights were seen in the skies. Some saw large stars with long bright tails, which they thought were like In-di-ans on horse back. Some said they had seen a long bright sword in the sky; and an In-di-an bow in the clouds; and a long scalp that fell from the north star. Then it seemed, too, as though the howl of the wolves came up close to their homes in the dead hour of the night, so that their flesh crept with fear.

In great crowds the whites left their farms and trades, and came to the large towns where they felt more safe. They thought their sins had brought on the war and all its ills. One of their great sins was that they wore long hair! They thought this did not please God, so they cut off their hair, and then set to work to do all they could to harm the poor Qua-kers, to whom for some time they had been quite kind.

All this would have been of no use if they had not sent out a large force of troops to fight the red men in their swamps. They were led by Jo-si-ah Wins-low. He went straight to where the Nar-ra-gan-sets were. It was in the heart of a swamp. A thick hedge shut them in. There was but one way to get through it and in the fort, and for three hours the Eng-lish tried to force their way through this small space. At last a few of the whites broke through a part of the hedge and fought the red men from the rear, and so won the day. Some of the red men fled in great haste to the woods. Some staid in the fort and were burnt to death when the white men set it on fire. Some lost their way in the deep snow drifts and soon froze to death.

The "Swamp Fight" did not bring the red men to terms. In a few weeks they were at their old work, with hearts of hate and hands swift to do deeds of blood. Some white men from Con-nec-ti-cut heard one day that the chief Ca-non-chet, the son of Mi-an-to-ni-mah, of whom you have heard, was near at hand, and they set out to catch him. He was a tall strong man, and they had hard work to keep on his track. But at last his foot slipped and he was caught. The whites tried to make friends with him, and to coax him to make terms of peace, and to give up some of his tribe who had done the most harm. But he said he would not be at peace with the white men, and would not give up to them one of the red men.

"We will fight to the last man," he said. "We will not be slaves of the white men."

The great chief was then led forth to be shot. He was told he might live if he would be at peace with the whites. This he would not do. He chose to die. "I like it well," he said in his quaint speech. "Now my heart is not soft, and I have said no words that would hurt the pride of an In-di-an chief. It is the time for me to die." Two red men took him to the woods and shot him, and his head was sent to Hart-ford.

Still there were no signs of peace.

All this while King Phil-ip was in the north, by the great lakes, where he had gone to try to get the tribes there to help his cause. But they had a great fear of the white men, and would not join Phil-ip, so he came back to his own land. One of his braves told him that the whites were sure to win, and urged Phil-ip to make terms of peace. The proud chief struck him dead with a blow from the small axe he bore. There could be no peace, he said, twixt the white men and the red.

But King Phil-ip lost heart when he saw the great tribes forced to make terms of peace. Most of his own brave men were dead, and he had to fly for his life. He laid in swamps, and hid in caves and dense woods as he tried to creep back to his old home. On the way he heard that his wife had been killed, and his young son sold as a slave, and in his great grief he cried out "My heart breaks! Now let me die!"

King Phil-ip was shot as he lay hid in a swamp, by one of his own men, and with his own gun.

This brought the war to

a close, which had been kept up for more than a year, and drove the red men quite out of New Eng-land.

I must now go back a ways and tell you how the Dutch came to find their way to A-mer-i-ca. Captain John Smith, of whom you have heard so much, had a friend, named Henry Hud-son, who went with him on his first trip to Vir-gin-ia. He thought, as Co-lum-bus did, that there must be a short cut to Chi-na and the East Indies right through A-mer-i-ca. There were no maps in those days to show the length and breadth of the land, and so it is not strange that men thought queer things.

But the Dutch were rich, and their ships were on all the seas, and as they thought it would be a fine thing to be the first to find out a short cut to Chi-na, they gave Hud-son a yacht called the Half Moon, in which he set sail for A-mer-i-ca. He took a new route, and when he came to Sandy-Hook, he was sure he had found the short cut he was in search of. He came up the Bay of New York and saw both shores green with grass and trees, and sweet scents were borne to him on each breeze. Red men came out to meet him, and sold him beans, and corn, and shell fish, and seemed glad to see the white men. Hud-son sailed up the stream which bears his name, but soon found it was not the right way to get to Chi-na, and the Half Moon had to turn back.

Then the Eng-lish gave him a ship, and this time he took a course that brought him to what is now known as Hud-son's Bay. He felt that he was right at last. But he sailed round and round the shores of the bay, and found there was but one way to get in or out. His ship froze fast in the ice, and had to stay there till spring. The crew blamed Hud-son for the hard life they had had in that cold place; so on the way back these bad men, who were worse than brutes, put him and his boy and eight more men in a small boat, and left them to drift on the wide, wide sea. That is the last that is known of this brave man.

But he had told the Dutch what a fine land he had seen when he went in the Half-Moon, and they at once sent ships to the spot and set up a trade in furs. It is said that they bought their furs by the pound, and as they had no weights such as are in use in these days, they told the In-di-ans that a Dutch man's hand weighed just one pound, and his foot two. And the red men thought it must be so. This may not be true, but it is a fact that the Dutch gave a few beads and things of no worth, for a large lot of rich furs which they could sell at a high price. When they saw a piece of land they liked they bought it, and gave the In-di-ans a string of beads, or a bit of gay silk, or a pipe for it. They went all round the coast to see if there were furs to sell, and if they found a good place to trade they put up a small fort, and left some one there to buy from the In-di-ans.

In a few years men left their farms in Hol-land and came to New York, which was then known as New Am-ster-dam. They had their farms in the woods and swamps where Broad-way now is, and let their cows and pigs run wild where the Cit-y Hall now stands.

The Dutch did not love to fight, but they were too fond of beer for their own good. They got drunk, and they made the In-di-ans drunk, and that was the chief cause of the wars that took place. The rum made brutes of the red men. The Dutch had to fly from the north. Their homes were burned down. Great tracts of land were laid waste.

For long years this state of things was kept up, and the Dutch had such a hard time that there is no doubt they wished they were back in Hol-land.

At the south end of Man-hat-tan a small band of Dutch men, with old Pe-ter Stuy-ve-sant at their head, kept the red men at bay. For a while they had things their own way; but in 1673 the Duke of York came from Eng-land and laid claim to New

Am-ster-dam, which since that time has been known as New York.

The old In-di-an name of Man-hat-tan, was *Man-a-hack-tan-i-enks*, which means " the place where they all get drunk."

CHAPTER VI.

TWO MEN OF PEACE.

The wars in the new and the old world were much talked of by old and young, and it was strange to hear of a boy who did not love to fight. Bad kings made bad laws, and good men found it hard to live in these days. Some of those who loved peace, and not war, formed a sect known as Qua-kers or "Friends."

These "Friends" had their own views of what was right and wrong, and were not much thought of in Eng-land at that time. They were bold in their speech, and though they thought it wrong to fight, thought it much worse to tell a lie.

Wil-liam Penn, the son of a rich man, was one of them. The king was in his debt, and to pay him gave Penn a tract of land in A-mer-i-ca, part of which was the home of Swedes who had bought it from the red men. Here Penn came to found a State where men could be free and live in peace. They were to make their own laws, and live up to them. Penn was just and kind with the red men, and soon made them his friends. He met the chief men of the tribes by a great elm-tree, where Phil-a-del-phia now is, and there made terms of "good faith and good will." Strong in truth and love he bent the fierce tribes of the Del-a-ware to his will. They vowed to live in love with Penn and his "Friends" as long as the moon and sun should last. And both sides kept their vows.

The fame of Penn and his men went to all lands. Grave and good men from all parts sought the home made for them in the New World. In three years Phil-a-del-phia was a large town, and the "Friends" there grew rich and wise and strong.

Some of the New Eng-land States did not treat the "Friends" well. Those who went to preach the word of the Lord there were sent back. Some were hung, some were whipped, some had their ears cut off. But the Qua-kers had friends at home, friends who stood near the king. The king took their part, and sent word to New Eng-land that this kind of war must stop at once. Since that time A-mer-i-cans have claimed the right to think as they choose, and to praise God as they please, and the Qua-kers are known all through the world as the true friends of love and peace.

I will tell you here of a wise man who was born in Bos-ton, and went on foot to Phil-a-del-phia when quite a lad. He was a poor boy, and had to work hard. He kept a shop where he sold ink and quill-pens, rags, soap, and such things. He bound books. He had a small hand-press, and knew how to set type so that he could print all the news of the day. This was his trade, of which he was so fond that he kept at it till he grew to be quite rich. He had not the least bit of mean pride or false shame.

As a boy he was fond of books and thought a great deal on what he read. This made him a wise man, whom it was safe to trust. He had thought for some time that the light that went with a flash through the sky could be made of use. So one day when there was a fierce storm he sent up a kite with a key tied to its string. He saw a spark come from the key, and knew that what he had thought out in his own mind was quite true. You will learn as you read on how that which he found out was put to great use, and how much A-mer-i-ca owes to Ben-ja-min Frank-lin. His great good sense made him a man of mark in his own time, and is the chief cause of the fame he has in these days.

The Swedes, who made their home in Phil-a-del-phia, were in great fear of

THE DECLARATION OF INDEPENDENCE.

the In-di-ans whose ways, speech, and dress were all so strange that they could not hope to make friends with them. The white men felt that they must be on guard all the time, or the foe would come and drive them out of the place. But one day it chanced that all the men Swedes went off to the woods and left their wives at home. It was soft-soap day; and I guess, if the truth were known, that was just why the men went off at that time.

The great pots were on the fire, and the soap was just at a boil, when word came that the In-di-ans were close at hand. What was to be done? They had no guns with which to fire on the foe, and no help was near. They ran with all speed to the church, that was built like a block-house, and took with them the soap that was as hot as fire and lye could make it. They made the door fast, and the red men, who knew how few and how weak they were, thought it would be no task to seize the "white squaws." So they stole up to the church, and as soon as they came near the "white squaws" slung out the soft-soap so that it went in their eyes and made them howl and dance in a queer kind of a way. The red men were scared by this kind of hot shot, and ran off as fast as they could go; and I guess the white men had a good laugh when they came home and heard how brave their wives had been.

CHAPTER VII.

FRENCH AND IN-DI-AN WARS.

The wars in the old world brought on wars in the new, and in 1754 the Eng-lish tried to drive the French from the lands they held in the New World. The French said they would keep that which they had found and had a right to, if they had to fight for it. So they built new forts, made their old ones more strong, and called the red men to their aid. The red men did not stand and fight as white men are taught to do, but hid near trees and rocks, or shot at the troops from shrubs or thick woods.

Gen-er-al Brad-dock, who was a brave man, would not let his troops fight in that way, so that they had the worst of it.

The first great fight with the French took place at Fort Du Quesne (*kane*) where Pitts-burg now stands. The fort was built of the trunks of trees, and near it were rude huts in which the French troops lived. Here and there was a patch of wheat or corn, which grew well in the rich soil.

Brad-dock had no doubt the fort would yield to him as soon as he came near it. So he led his men on through a road twelve feet wide with high ground in front and on both sides. Soon a war-whoop burst from the woods. The troops were shot down by a foe they could not see. For three hours the fight was kept up. Then the men broke ranks and fled. Braddock had a bad wound. "Who would have thought it?" he said in a low voice, as his men bore him from the field he was so sure he would win. These were the last words he spoke, and he died in two or three days.

He had been warned by such wise men as George Wash-ing-ton and Ben-ja-min Frank-lin, but he gave no heed to their words, and so met his fate.

Up to this time Eng-land and France had been at peace. Now they were at strife, and the flames of war spread far and wide. Blood was shed on land and on sea, and hearts were full of woe. Brit-ish troops were sent to A-mer-i-ca to fight the French there. Que-bec was one of the strong points held by the French. To this place came a fleet in charge of Gen-e-ral Wolfe.

There were two towns, one on the beach, and one on the cliff. Wolf fired bomb-shells at the town on the beach, which was soon laid low. The town on the cliff was too far off for him to reach in this way. At last he hit on a plan so bold that the French did not dream of it. The shore for miles and miles was searched with care. A spot was found whence a path wound up to the cliff. At this point Wolfe could land his men and lead them to the Heights of A-bra-ham. Once there they would turn out the French, take Que-bec, or die where they stood.

At night the troops went down the stream in boats to the place known as Wolfe's Cave. All through the night they scaled the tall cliffs, and with the aid of the ship's crew drew up a few guns. When it was light, the whole force was drawn up on the plain. As soon as he could, Mont-calm went out with his French troops to meet the Brit-ish. The fight was fierce on both sides but did not last long. The French were put to flight.

Both Mont-calm and Wolfe fell in the strife. While Wolfe lay on the ground he heard some one say:—

"They fly! they fly!"

"Who fly?" said he.

"The French," they told him.

"Then" said the brave man, "I die in peace;" and he died.

The French lost heart when they lost Que-bec, and the long war was closed in 1763. The King of France gave up all right to the lands he had laid claim to in that part of the New World, and no one but King George could make laws that should rule A-mer-i-ca.

In all parts of A-mer-i-ca the French were ill-used by the Brit-ish king. They were torn from their homes and friends, and some of them were left to die on a cold, bleak coast, where they were told to wait for the ships to take them back to their own dear France.

It is said that an I-rish-man, named John-son, wrote to Eng-land of the brave way in which he had fought the French at Crown Point. He was not a brave man at all and there were those in New Eng-land who knew that he had not told the whole truth. But in Old Eng-land they thought it must be true, and he was made Sir Wil-liam John-son, and had more praise than was his due. He was a vain man and fond of fine clothes, and was quite proud of the rich suits that were sent him from Eng-land, all trimmed with lace as was the style in those days.

A Mo-hawk chief saw these gay clothes, and thought how much he should like to own them. He went up to Sir Wil-li-am, and said he had had a dream.

"Ah?" said Sir Wil-li-am, "and what did you dream?"

"I dreamt that you gave me one of those rich suits of clothes."

John-son was as shrewd as the In-di-an. He took one of the fine suits and gave it to the chief, who went off much pleased.

In a few days John-son met the chief, and said to him.

"By-the-by, I have had a dream."

"Ah!" said the In-di-an, "what was it?"

"Why, that you gave me that tract of land," a fine large tract on the Mo-hawk Riv-er.

The In-di-an saw how he was caught. But he gave the land, and said, with a sigh, "I dream no more with you, Sir Wil-li-am, you dream too hard."

CHAPTER VIII.

THE CAUSE OF A GREAT WAR.

Those who sat on thrones thought that they had the best right to make laws and to rule men. But the men who came to the New World had come to be free from the hard laws that kings made. It did not suit them to be at the beck and call of those who were not wise or good, and they found in their new homes that it was best for them to make their own laws. They must have free speech as well as free air. They said the king's laws were not just. The war with France had cost a great deal, and King George said it was but right that the men in A-mer-i-ca should pay it back. So he made a law that no note, bond, or deed was good that had not the king's seal on it.

The "Stamp Act" was passed in 1765. The A-mer-i-cans thought it a mean trick to make them pay a tax in this way, and they said they would not use the stamps at all. They got up a "strike," just as men do now-a-days when laws do not please them, and made such a stir that the king said they need not be bound by the "Stamp Act."

This gave them great joy, but it did not last long. They made up their minds they would not eat, drink, or wear the least thing that came from Eng-land. When the king found they would not buy goods that had a tax on them, he was wise and took it off. But one tax he left; and that was the tax on tea. The king made up his mind that this tax should be paid, and so sent ship loads of troops to see that his will was done. Three pence on a pound did not seem much of a tax, and had it been a just tax it would have been paid.

The troops came to all the large towns, which were soon filled with red-coats, who had to be fed and cared for by the men who could not but hate the sight of them. Mobs met in the streets, and there was now and then a fight with the king's troops. This was in the year 1770. In March of that year the mob grew too bold, and bore so hard on the king's troops that the troops had to fire on the crowd. Ten or more were killed, and blood stained the snow and ice that lay in the streets.

This was the "Bos-ton Mas-sa-cre" which made our men hate the king and all his laws still more than they had done.

One day ships that were known to have tea on board showed their tall masts in the bay. It was Sun-day and the men of Bos-ton were strict in their views, and did no work on the Lord's-day. But old rules had to give way to this new case, which must be met at once.

Sam-u-el Ad-ams was the true king of Bos-ton at that time. He was the first to see what must be done. "We are free," he said, "and want no king!"

Men were wild with rage. If the ships came to land, the tea would be sold! What must be done? All talk was vain. Ad-ams stood up in the church and told them if they would be free, now was the time to strike the blow. With a wild shout the men ran out of the church. Some of them, drest to look like In-di-ans, went in great haste to the wharf, each one with an axe in his hand. They went on board the ships, brought the chests of tea on deck, broke them up and threw them in the bay.

So still was the crowd that not a sound was heard but the stroke of the axe, and the splash of the chests as they fell in the sea. This is what A-mer-i-ca did. It was for Eng-land to make the next move.

The king said that no

kind of goods should be sent to Bos-ton. This did more harm than good, as it showed the men there how mean the Brit-ish were. They would have to fight to get free from such men, and such laws.

CHAPTER IX.

THE FIRST FIGHT.

When our men saw that the king meant to force them to do as he said and to keep his laws, they went to work to learn the art of war. They were led by wise and good men.

The first fight took place at Lex-ing-ton in Mas-sa-chu-setts in the spring of 1775.

Gen-er-al Gage who had charge of the king's troops, had heard that a lot of guns and things that were used in war, were stored in Con-cord, a few miles from Bos-ton. He would seize them in the king's name, and he thought that not a hint had got out of what he meant to do.

But sharp men were on the watch. Gen-er-al War-ren, who fell at Bun-ker Hill, at once sent Paul Reu-vere to spread the news. He rode like the wind through Bos-ton, and then took a boat to Charles-town. He was none too soon. Gen-er-al Gage heard that his plans had been found out, and at once sent word that no one should leave Bos-ton. It was too late. A small band of men in their farm clothes met the red-coats on the field of Lex-ing-ton, but were told by John Par-ker who led them that they should not be the first to fire.

Ma-jor Pit-cairn rode up, and with an oath bade the king's troops to fire at once, and his gun sent the first shot at those brave men, who did not fear to die in so just a cause.

No Eng-lish blood was shed. Cheer on cheer went up from the ranks of the red-coats who took up their march to Con-cord, which is six miles from Lex-ing-ton.

Our men had left their farms and were drawn up on a hill, from whence they could see all that was done by the foe. The red-coats held the bridge, while some of their men went this way and that to search for the guns and such things that were kept at Con-cord. But these had all been hid where the red-coats could not find them. The men on the hill kept a close watch, and soon they saw a cloud of smoke rise from the spot where their homes were. The lives of those they held most dear were at stake. What could they do? The wolf was in the fold where their lambs were! With hearts on fire the brave men fell in line, went down the hill, and took the road that led to the bridge. They were charged not to fire the first shot.

As soon as the red-coats saw them they went to work to tear up the planks of the bridge. Our men made more haste. Then the king's-troops fired, at first one or two shots, which did no harm. Then a few more by which two men were hurt; then a fierce charge, and two of our men fell dead.

"Fire! For God's sake, fire!" cried Ma-jor John But-trick, of Con-cord, as he gave a wild leap in the air. His men did not wait. The fight was a short and sharp one. The red-coats had to give up the bridge, and make their way back to Bos-ton. They met with great loss in the fight; some of their best men were killed, and they were shot at all the way on the road as they ran, so that they had no chance to rest.

The day was hot, the march long, and they had had to work hard, and with no food. Fresh troops, led by Lord Per-cy, were sent from Bos-ton to their aid, and met them near the place where they had shot down our men that morn and it is said, that when they lay down to rest "their tongues hung out of their mouths like those of a dog who has had a hard chase."

The news rang through the land that blood had been spilt. Men on horse-back rode hard through high-ways and by-ways to spread the tale. All men felt that the hour had come, and in all the States there was a rush to arms.

Down in Con-nec-ti-cut

there was an old man at work in the field with his plough. His name was Is-ra-el Put-nam. He had fought with the red men in his young days, and had been near death at their hands. Once he had been bound to a tree, and the In-di-ans had their arms up to strike the blow that would kill him, when he was found by some of his friends who had gone out in search of him, and his life was saved.

As the old man drove his plough through the field some one told him of the fight at Lex-ing-ton. He took his horse from the plough, sent word home that he had gone to Bos-ton, and rode with all speed to the A-mer-i-can camp. On a neck of land, close by Bos-ton, there are two low hills, one known as Bun-ker Hill, and one as Breed's Hill. Our men made up their minds to fight the Brit-ish from this point. There was no time to lose. It was said that Gen-er-al Gage meant to put a large force of his men on the heights on the 18th of June. He was too late. On the 16th, just ere the sun went down in the west, our men met on Cam-bridge Com-mon to ask God to bless them in what they had planned to do.

Col-o-nel (*kurnel*) Pres-cott, who had fought in the wars with the French, was in charge of our troops; and Put-nam was with him, to be of use where he could.

With hearts that were

brave to do and die, the men set forth on their march. Not a word was said. Their feet scarce made a sound. Their way led them near the guns of the Eng-lish ships, but they were not seen or heard. The night was warm and still. They reach the hill-top. How swift they work to build their fort of earth and logs! With what care they must use their spades, lest one stroke on a stone should tell the tale, and spoil all!

When Gen-er-al Gage looked out on the heights the next day at dawn, he saw strong earth-works, and swarms of men in arms, where he had been wont to see a broad sweep of green grass on which no foot had trod. A tall form went back and forth on the top of the earth-works. It was Pres-cott.

"Will he fight?" asked Gage of one who stood near by. "Yes, sir," said the man to whom he spoke, "to the last drop of his blood!"

A plan was made at once. The Brit-ish were to march straight up the hill and drive off the A-mer-i-cans. It was not thought that our men could stand the shock, as it was well known they were more used to peace than to war, and had but few guns and balls to fight with. At noon the red-coats left Bos-ton in their small boats, and were soon at Charles-town. The A-mer-i-cans kept a close watch on them from the hill-top, and felt no fear. From all the heights in the range of Bos-ton, on hills, house-tops, and church spires, crowds of A-mer-i-cans stood to watch the fight.

It was no light task for the Brit-ish to climb that hill. The day was hot, the grass was long and thick, and the load each man bore made his step slow. While yet a long way off the red-coats fired their guns as if to wake up the foe. Not a shot came back from the A-mer-i-can lines. "Aim low," said Put-nam, "and wait till you see the whites of their eyes."

The Eng-lish were quite near the works when Pres-cott told his men to fire. The A-mer-i-cans could shoot to a hair's breadth. Their aim was true, and when they fired not a shot missed its mark. Men fell from the Brit-ish ranks by scores. The troops fled down the hill. Then with fresh strength they climb the heights, to be sent back with great loss. Now at the foot of the hill they strip off their great coats, that they may have a hand-to-hand fight. Up they go and climb the walls that they may take the fort. The A-mer-i-cans met them with stones and the butt-ends of their guns but the Brit-ish were too strong for them. They soon drove the brave band down the hill, and made them cross the neck to Cam-bridge, while the Eng-lish ships raked them with grape-shot as they ran. They had done their work. It was true the red-coats had won the day; but our men had found out that with the help of some slight field-works, green hands, fresh from the farm or field, who had had no chance to drill, were a match for the best troops that Eng-land could send.

I will tell you here of two brave deeds done by Is-ra-el Put-nam. For a long time he, and those who dwelt near him, had been ill used by a fierce wolf, which at night would kill their sheep and goats, and lambs and kids. Put-nam made a plan for five men to take turns and hunt the wolf till they could take her life. It was known that she had lost two of her toes in a steel trap, and so made one short track and one long one. By this they could trace her course in the light snow. At last they drove her to a den three miles from Put-nam's house. The folks from all round, came with dogs, guns, straw, and fire to fight this fierce foe, and to force her from the den. From ten at morn till ten at night they kept at work. The hounds came back with bad wounds, and ran as far as they could from the old wolf's teeth.

Put-nam tried to make his dog go in the cave, but in vain. He asked his black man to go down and shoot the wolf; but the black man would not. Then the brave man said, with a flash of his eye, that if no one else would go he would, for he feared the wolf would run off through some hole in the rocks.

He took some strips of birch bark that he might have light in the deep dark cave, and scare the wolf as well, for wild beasts shrink from the sight of fire. Then he threw off his coat and vest, tied a long rope to his legs, by which he might be pulled back when he gave the sign, and with a torch in his hand went head first in the den. The place was as still as the grave. He crept on his hands till he came face to face with the great red eye-balls of the wolf, who sat at the end of the cave. At the sight of fire she gnashed her teeth, and gave a low growl.

As soon as Put-nam found out where the beast was he gave a kick and was at once drawn out of the cave. Those at the mouth of the den had heard the growl and thought, of course, that the wolf had sprung at their friend and would eat him up. They drew him out so fast that his clothes were torn from his back, and his flesh was much bruised. Put-nam set his clothes right, put a charge of nine buck-shot in his gun, and with that in his right hand and a torch in his left, he went once more in the den. As he drew near the wolf she snapped her teeth, put her head down, and crouched to spring when Put-nam raised his gun took a sure aim, and fired. Stunned with the shock, and choked by the smoke, he was at once drawn out to the fresh

THE SURRENDER OF CORNWALLIS

air. When he had had some rest, and the smoke was out of the cave, he went down for the third time. Once more he came in sight of the wolf. He put the torch to her nose. She did not move. Then he knew she was dead ; so he took hold of her ears, gave the rope a kick, for it was still tied round his legs, and with great shouts of joy both the man and the wolf were drawn out through the mouth of the cave.

CHAPTER X.

GEORGE WASH-ING-TON.

George Wash-ing-ton was born in Vir-gin-ia, in the year 1732. As a boy he had a keen love of the truth, and would scorn to tell a lie. He was so calm and just when at school that the boys would call on him to make peace when they were at strife. He knew how to rule his own heart, and grew up to be a wise and good man. When he saw it was right to do a thing, he did that thing at once. He had a strong mind, a strong will, and a strong heart; and he had a great work to do in the world. He was born to rule. Two weeks from the time the fight took place at Bun-ker Hill, Wash-ing-ton was sent for to be the *Com-man-der-in-chief* of our men. Though brave at heart they were green in war, and had but few of the things most used at such times.

The first thing Wash-ing-ton did was to teach them the art of war. Some thought he ought to rush right on the Brit-ish in Bos-ton. But he did not think so. He kept them so close in the town all those long cold days that they were most starved to death.

At last, they were in such a strait that Gen-er-al Howe, the Brit-ish chief was forced to ask Wash-ing-ton to let him and his troops leave Bos-ton. This Wash-ing-ton was glad to do. Then the Eng-lish set sail for Hal-i-fax in March, 1776, and the A-mer-i-cans marched in to Bos-ton to the great joy of all the folks there. The reign of King George in that place was at an end. While the Brit-ish were still in Bos-ton, Howe sent a force of ships to lay siege to Charles-ton, in South Car-o-li-na. But Wash-ing-ton found out his plan, and sent Gen-er-al Lee to meet him.

When the Brit-ish fleet came in sight of Charles-ton it was found that a strong fort had been built of earth and logs, so that the ships could not land. The men on board sent bomb-shells at the fort, which sank in the soft wood so that not much harm was done. But the shot from the fort swept the decks of the Brit-ish ships.

When the fight was at its height, a brave deed was done by a young man named Jas-per. One of the balls had cut down the staff which held the flag the men in the fort were so proud of. As soon as Jasper saw it he sprang from the breast-works, seized the flag and put it back in its place, while round him the balls fell like hail-stones.

For a whole day the Brit-ish kept up the fight. But they could not take the fort. So they gave it up, and set sail. The fort was called Fort Moul-trie, as that was the name of the brave man who kept it from the foe.

When the Brit-ish left Bos-ton, Wash-ing-ton had a fear that they meant to go to New York, so he made up his mind to move his own troops to that place. He left some of his men in Bos-ton so that the Brit-ish should not come back and take it, and then set sail for New York. Then he set his men to work to build forts near the town, and on Long Is-land, and up the Hud-son, for the war was to be kept up till the whole of A-mer-i-ca was free from Eng-lish rule. What took place on the 4th of Ju-ly, 1776? I will tell you.

On that day our men drew up an act, called "*The Dec-la-ra-tion* of *In-de-pen-dence.*" Thom-as Jef-fer-son wrote it, and it was full of grand words that rang out like a chime of bells.

The *Con-ti-nent-al Con-gress* was made up of wise men who made the laws by which A-mèr-i-cans chose to be ruled. They met in Phil-a-del-phia, in a room in In-de-pen-dence Hall. When the word went forth that the *Dec-la-ra-tion* had been signed and sealed, the old bell-man seized the tongue of the great bell and swung it back and forth with all his might.

> At each loud stroke
>   The old bell spoke,
> "We will not wear
>   King George's Yoke!
>
> "From South to North
>   Our cry shall be,
> From this time forth
>   We shall be free!"
>
> So loud the peal,
>   So great the stroke,
> That in its joy
>   The big bell broke.

This is true. And when you go to Phil-a-del-phia you must ask to see the great bell that rang out such a wild peal of joy on that day; and if you look on one side of it you will see the large crack that was made, so that it could ring no more.

I must tell you what the folks in New York did. In that town stood a cast of King George III. It was made of lead. In one hand he held a kind of sword; and on his head he wore a crown. When the news of the *Dec-la-ra-tion* of *In-de-pen-dence* reached New York a great crowd ran to one spot, and the cry was heard "Down with it!—down with it!" and soon a rope was put round its neck, and the lead King

George came down to the ground. Then it was cut all to bits, and made up in balls with which to kill the troops that had been sent from Eng-land to fight the A-mer-i-cans.

CHAPTER XI.

DARK DAYS.

In the fall of 1776 a deep gloom spread through the land.

Gen-er-al Howe had his troops in camp on Stat-en-Is-land a few miles from New York, and in full view of Brook-lyn.

Wash-ing-ton sent a strong force to hold the heights of Brook-lyn and to throw up earth-works in front of the town.

But the Eng-lish had more men, and the field was lost to the A-mer-i-cans, who fled to Har-lem, nine miles from New York. But the Eng-lish ships swept up the Hud-son and got in the front and rear of Wash-ing-ton and his troops. The Brit-ish took Fort Wash-ing-ton, which was so great a loss that it made Wash-ing-ton shed tears.

He led his men to New Jer-sey. The ground as they went was stained with their blood. The most of them felt that their cause was lost. They were in sore need. The red-coats, though close in the rear of Wash-ing-ton, could not catch up to him. In this way he got down to the Del-a-ware, which he had to cross to get to Penn-syl-va-nia. As he took care to take all the boats with him, the Brit-ish could not cross when they got there. The stream was full of ice, and it was hard work for men who were not half clad or half fed. But they did it, and kept on their way by land as soon as they reached the shore.

At the close of the year Wash-ing-ton had a chance to clip the wings of the Brit-ish at Trent-on and Prince-ton so that they fell back and gave up a large part of New Jer-sey.

The next year, that is in 1777, our men lost ground; and dark were the days they spent at Val-ley Forge.

They had not much to eat, and their clothes hung in rags. Some of them had no shoes, and their steps could be traced by the blood-marks they left in the snow. They had to keep as warm as they could in their small huts, or round the camp-fires, and if the fire of love for their own land had not burned strong in their hearts they could not have stood it at all.

At this time a new force came to the aid of these brave men. France was at heart the friend of A-mer-i-ca, but did not dare to take a bold part in the war. But she let one of her bright young chiefs cross the sea to help the cause for which they fought. His name was La-Fay-ette. He was a young man of great wealth, and in a high place at the French court. He left his young wife, his home, and all he held dear, to cast his lot with those who were in great need of this kind of cheer. Wash-ing-ton met him with tears of joy in his eyes, and gave him a place on his staff. He put new strength in the troops, and made their cause his own. For this he holds a high place in the love of all true A-mer-i-cans. When the war was at an end, and A-mer-i-ca free, he went back to France. In the year 1826, when La-fay-ette was an old man he came to see once more the land he had helped to save. The fame of his good and brave deeds will last till the end of time.

In the spring of 1777, Gen-er-al Bur-goyne set out from Can-a-da with a fine lot of troops. He was to go south and be met at Al-ba-ny by a Brit-ish force which was to march up from New York. This was a grand plan to cut our lines in two. He marched far in the New Eng-land States. As he drew near men took down their guns from the walls and went to the front. They had not much skill in the art of war, but they had firm hearts and a sure aim. It was not long ere the Brit-ish found out they were caught as in a net.

Our men were at the front and rear and on all sides. In grief and shame the red-coats laid down their arms to a crowd of rough ill-dressed men, most of whom wore their guns slung on their backs! It was a great blow to Eng-land.

Near the same time Gen-er-al Howe tried to cross Wash-ing-ton's path and take Phil-a-del-phia, then the chief town of all the States. As he could not get there by land he went back to New York and set sail from that place. Our men were drawn up on the banks of the Bran-dy-wine, but though they fought well the red-coats were too strong for them, and drove them from the field. In a few days a Brit-ish force with Lord Corn-wal-lis at its head made its way to Phil-a-del-phia. The band played "God save the King." The day was bright. The streets were gay; and there were some folks in the town who were full of joy, and glad to see King George's men. They were met as friends and not as foes.

Said wise Ben Frank-lin, "Gen-er-al Howe did not take Phil-a-del-phia; Phil-a-del-phia took Gen-er-al Howe."

I must tell you of a great feat done by Gen-er-al Put-nam, or "old Put" as he was called, while the red-coats made war through New Eng-land. They robbed and set on fire the towns they went through, and at last came to Horse-neck, which is on the

Sound a few miles from New York. Gen-er-al Put-nam was at Horse-neck with a small force of men and two large guns. The Brit-ish had more men, but less pluck.

"Old Put" was a bold man. He set his guns on a hill near the church; and as the red-coats came up the guns were fired. At length the foe came so close that he told his men to run and hide in a swamp near by. He was on horse-back, and the hill was so steep that no horse could go down it but by the road on which the red-coats were. But the man who had the wit to snare a wolf, was not the one to be caught in a trap. He saw some stone steps that had been laid so that those in the vale could get up to the church which was on the hill. It is life or death, thought Put-nam, and down he rode at break-neck speed. On came the Brit-ish. They were sure of him. But when they reached the spot they saw "old Put" a long way off. They did not dare to go down the steps, so they shot at him, and would have killed him if they could. But one ball came near him, and that went through his hat.

CHAPTER XII.

THE CLOSE OF THE WAR.

The French had shown such good will to our men, that Frank-lin was sent to ask their aid. The King of France said he would help with ships, men, and gold, and he was as good as his word. This brought much cheer to the hearts of the A-mer-i-cans. When Eng-land heard what France meant to do, she tried her best to make peace. But it was too late.

From the year 1779 the war went on in the South, where much blood was spilt. There were loss and gain on both sides, but at last the Brit-ish troops were forced back to Charles-ton, where they stayed till the close of the war.

We now come to a dark page and a dark plot by which, if it had not been found out, A-mer-i-ca would have lost all she had fought so hard to win. This was a plan to place West-Point in the hands of the Brit-ish. West-Point was a strong fort on the Hud-son which was in charge of Gen-er-al Ar-nold. The Brit-ish knew it was worth their while to get this post, so they sent word to Ar-nold that he might have a large sum in gold if he would give it up. This he meant to do if he had not been found out. No true man will take a bribe of this sort. Wash-ing-ton bade him leave the post, and he went off in a great rage.

Then he came back full of grief for the wrong he had done, and said he meant from that hour to do right, and begged to be sent back to his post at West-Point. But his heart was black; his thoughts were base; and Wash-ing-ton, who had a kind heart, did wrong to trust him. As soon as he was once more in charge of West-Point he wrote to Sir Hen-ry Clin-ton, who was with the Brit-ish in New York, to send some one to whom he could give up the fort.

Ma-jor An-dré was sent up the Hud-son in a sloop of war, named the Vul-ture.

The night was pitch dark when he left the boat and went to the place where he was to meet Ar-nold. Day broke ere their talk came to an end. It was not safe for An-dré to be seen. The ship from which he had come lay in full view. Would that he could reach her! He must make his way back to New York by land as best he could. A pass from Ar-nold took him through the A-mer-i-can lines, and then he drew a free breath, and felt no more fear.

He came to a small stream; thick woods on the right and on the left made the night seem more dark. All at once three armed men came out from the trees and bade him halt. From the dress of one of them An-dré thought he was with friends. Poor An-dré! He soon found out they were not friends at all. They searched him, and at first nought was found. Then one of the men said, " Boys, I am still in doubt. His boots must come off."

André's face fell. His boots were searched, and Ar-nold's sketch of West-Point was found. The men knew then that he was a spy. Word was at once sent to Wash-ing-ton who was then at West-Point. As soon as Ar-nold heard that his plot was found out he fled in great haste to a Brit-ish man-of-war. An-dré was tried, and by the rules of war he had to be hung. It was a sad fate for so young and so good a man, and gave great pain to all those who took part in the act. Had it been Ar-nold, no tears would have been shed. This bad man, who was to blame for An-dré's death, made his way to New York, and took sides with the Brit-ish. When the war came to an end he went to Eng-land, where in 1801 he died; and in the whole wide world there was no one who had the least love for the man, or would shed a tear at his grave. He won the hate of Eng-lish-men as well as A-mer-i-cans, and I would warn all boys not to do as *Ben-e-dict Ar-nold* did.

We come now to the fight which brought the war to a close. It took place at York-town in Vir-gin-ia, in the year 1781.

Wash-ing-ton was near New York and thought to march on that place. But he changed his plan, and went in great haste to fight Lord Corn-wal-lis and to lay siege to York-town. He had the French to help him; and their men-of-war shut up the bay so that the Brit-ish could not get out to sea in their own boats. A sharp fire of shot and shell was kept up in front and rear. The red-coats were shut in on all sides, and met with great loss. They had but few guns; and their shot gave out. For more than ten days the fight was kept up, and the Brit-ish did all that brave men could do to hold the fort. But the red-hot shot of the French set fire to their ships. Their earth-works were torn up by the fire of our troops who came up with such speed that the foe lost all hope.

Corn-wal-lis sent out a flag of truce. The Brit-ish laid down their arms. Peace had come at last, and the joy of A-mer-i-ca knew no bounds.

It was eight years since the first blood was shed at Lex-ing-ton. Thus long had our men fought, and bled, and borne all sorts of ills to win what was well worth all it cost them. Now they were free; and Eng-land was the same to them as all the rest of the world—"in peace, a friend; in war, a foe."

By the end of the year 1783 the last red-coat had left our shores; and our troops went back to their homes.

Wash-ing-ton had won the love of all hearts. The men who had fought with him were loath to leave him. It was a sad time. Strong men shed tears when Wash-ing-ton bade them good-by. Tears were in his own eyes. He would take no pay for what he had done. His troops would have made him king, but he had no wish to be on a throne. He was sick of war and of a life of care, and glad to go back to his farm and spend the rest of his days in peace.

CHAPTER XIII.

ON SHIP AND SHORE.

The war left A-mer-i-ca in a sad state. Towns and fields had been laid waste by fire. All the arts of peace had been made to stop. There was a big debt to be paid. Laws must be made for those who were now free from the rule of Eng-land. It took wise and good men three or four years to work out a plan that would meet the case.

They had need of some wise and good man at the head. It was the vote of the States that George Wash-ing-ton was the man to fill the place. At the same time they cast their votes for two men, so that in case the chief died there would be some one to take his place. George Wash-ing-ton and John Ad-ams were the two they chose, and on the fourth of March, 1789. Wash-ing-ton took his place as the chief of the band who were to make the laws of A-mer-i-ca. He served for eight years, and did so well for the U-ni-ted States —as they were now called— that it was said of him "He was first in war—first in peace." It was the wish of all that he should serve a third term, but he would not, and in the year 1799 he died, and his death was felt to be a great loss.

John Ad-ams was chief for one term—of four years—from 1797 to 1801.

Thomas Jef-fer-son two terms, from 1801 to 1809.

James Mad-i-son two terms, from 1809 to 1817.

While Mad-i-son was chief, and our land had been at peace not quite a score of years, it had to go to war once more with Eng-land. It is called "the war of 1812," as it took place in that year. This was the cause of it: Eng-land said that she had a right to search our ships, to see if they had on board of them men who ought to serve Great Brit-ain The search was not just, and men were seized and made to serve a flag they did not love. Some of our men would not let a search be made on their ships and much blood was shed. These deeds brought on the war which was kept up on the sea and on the land. Our men could not do much on the land, but with their ships they kept up a brave fight and had good luck on the sea, and took five Brit-ish ships-of-war.

The first fight was with the Con-sti-tu-tion and Guer-ri-ere. The last named was a Brit-ish ship. So fierce was the fire of shot from our side that in half an hour there was not a spar left on the deck of the Guer-ri-ere; and the next day she was blown up, as there was no way in which she could be towed to port.

The next one was that of the Mac-e-do-ni-an and U-ni-ted States. The brave Com-mo-dore De-ca-tur had charge of our ship, which took the Eng-lish ship as a prize.

The Ja-va was next caught by the Con-sti-tu-tion, and the Pea-cock by the Hor-net. The Pea-cock had such great holes made in her hull by the balls sent from the Hor-net by our men, that she sank with some of her men on board.

Two Eng-lish ships lay off Bos-ton in the warm months of the year 1813. In the bay the A-mer-i-can ship Ches-a-peake had lain for some months. Broke sent off one of his ships, and sent word to Law-rence that he would match his

FIGHT BETWEEN THE CONSTITUTION AND GUERRIERE.

ship, the Shan-non, with the Ches-a-peake. Then he stood close in to the shore to wait for his foe to come forth. Crowds went on house-top and hill to see the fight. Not a shot was fired till the ships were so near that the men could see the eyes of those they meant to kill. The fire of the Brit-ish soon told on our ship. Her sails are torn; her masts fall; her deck is swept by the balls sent from the huge guns. The ships are now side by side. The Shan-non still fires grape-shot from two of her guns. Broke leaps on board the Ches-a-peake whose deck is wet with blood, tears down the flag, and the fight is at an end in less than half an hour. If it is sad for us to read of such things, what must it have been for those who took part in them?

Law-rence had his death-wound in this fight, and with his last breath he said to his men. "Don't give up the ship!" This has been since that day the watch word of A-mer-i-can tars.

I will now tell you of a fight that took place on Lake E-rie, in the fall of 1813, in which our men won the day. The A-mer-i-can fleet of nine ships was in charge of Com-mo-dore Per-ry. The Brit-ish had but six ships, but these had more guns than ours.

Per-ry's flag-ship was the Law-rence, and the words "Don't give up the ship"—the last that brave man spoke—were on the flag that was sent up as a sign that the fight was to set in. The Brit-ish ships point most of their guns at the Law-rence. For two hours they pour the shot at her till her guns have no place to rest, and she lies a wreck on the wave. There are but few of her crew who are not hurt. It is clear to Com-mo-dore Per-ry that he must leave his ship and make his way, if he can, to one of those that lie near.

He took his flag with him, and in a small buat made his way to the Ni-ag-a-ra, while the whole of the Brit-ish fleet kept up the fire of their guns in hopes to stop his course.

In less than half an hour Per-ry took the whole of the Brit-ish fleet, and then sat down and wrote of it in these words; "We have met the foe, and they are ours."

For three years the war was kept up. The A-mer-i-cans were sick of it. The Brit-ish lost more than they gained. Men from both sides met at Ghent, and made terms of peace.

A Brit-ish sloop-of-war brought the news to New York; and none too soon. The fight at New Or-leans took place while the ship was on the sea. It was won by the A-mer-i-cans, led by Gen-er-al Jack-son. He was rough in his ways, but his men were fond of him, and they gave him the pet name of "Old Hick-o-ry."

The cry of "Peace!

peace!" rang through the streets. Fires were lit. Bos-ton was wild with joy. Ships that had long lain at her wharves were soon sent out to sea, to trade, and not to make war.

It was a glad time. New States were formed. Men came in swarms from the Old World, and went to the west to make new homes.

On the fourth of March, 1817, James Mon-roe, was sworn in as chief of our land, and he made a tour through most of the States, to learn their needs and their growth, that his rule might be a wise one.

In 1825 John Quin-cy Ad-ams was made chief, by a large vote, for a term of four years. His rule was one of peace. As there were more men to choose from, those who had a right to vote took sides. Each had its own friend.

In 1829 the votes were cast for John Quin-cy Ad-ams and An-drew Jack-son. When they came to count them, Jack-son had the most, so he was made chief on the 4th of March. His home was in Ten-nes-see.

Jack-son was a man of strong will, and did some things that did not please some of the folks. But he was much liked, and held the place of chief for two terms.

In 1837 Mar-tin Van Bu-ren was made chief for a term of four years. By this time some of the States felt that Jack-son had not been the right kind of man for them, and the most that Van Bu-ren could do was to try to keep the peace.

In 1841 Gen-er-al Wil-li-am Hen-ry Har-ri-son was made chief with great pomp. His friends had hopes that his rule would prove a great joy to the land. He was a brave man, and a good man; one that had been tried and found as true as steel. All was bright and fair. But just one month from the day he was made chief the old man died. He was sick but a few days. John Ty-ler took his place, but he did not please those who had cast their votes for Har-ri-son.

In the band that were kept near the chief, to aid him in time of need, were such men as Hen-ry Clay, and Dan-i-el Web-ster, of whom you may have heard. These men had large brains, and large hearts, and when they got up to speak it was worth while to hear what they had to say. A-mer-i-ca was proud of these men, and is to this day.

CHAPTER XIV.

WHAT TOOK PLACE IN MEX-I-CO AND CAL-I-FOR-NIA.

In 1845 James K. Polk was sworn in. He had to take an oath, as did all the rest of the chiefs, that he would be true, and would serve his land the best he knew how. In his term a war with Mex-i-co broke out. The cause of this war was three-fold. In the first place Mex-i-co did not want Tex-as to join the States, which she did in 1845, and was full of ill-will. In the next place those States in the South that held slaves did not like Mex-i-co at all. I will tell you why. The Pope of Rome would have no slaves in Mex-i-co, and so if a slave could make his way there he would be a free man. I will tell you more of the Slave States by-and-by.

In the third place Mex-i-co was not sure how big Tex-as ought to be, and was at strife all the time with the U-ni-ted States, who wished to have men sent from both sides to fix the line. This did not suit Mex-i-co, and so there was a war.

In the spring of 1846, Gen-er-al Zach-a-ry Tay-lor was sent with a force to the Ri-o Gran-de, which our men claimed as the line that bound Tex-as on the south and south-west. Two fights took place at this point, both of which were won by Gen-er-al Tay-lor. This gave great joy to all the States; and a large force was at once raised, and Gen-er-al Win-field Scott put at its head.

In the mean-time Gen-er-al Tay-lor beat San-ta An-na in two more fights —at Mon-te-rey and Bu-e-na Vis-ta. At the last named place San-ta An-na had four or five times more troops than Gen-er-al Tay-lor. In the last fight San-ta An-na fled in such haste that he left his cork leg!

Gen-er-al Tay-lor was fond of a joke, and did not mind a bit of fun now and then. He was rough in his speech and had a quick wit, and that is how he won the name of "Old Rough and Read-y." He knew just what to say and what to do when the time came for him to speak and act, and though a man of war had a great big heart, and more friends than foes.

At one time, in the midst of a great fight with the Mex-i-cans, the balls came thick and fast quite near the place where Tay-lor stood with some of his staff. The men did not like this kind of fun, and would duck their heads when a ball went by. The old Gen-er-al saw this, and said "Don't dodge! Brave men should not dodge!" It was not long ere a big ball came so near the old man's nose that it made him start back. At this his men set up a loud laugh.

A flush of shame lit the old man's face, and he felt that he was in a fix. Then a smile broke through the cloud, and with a light laugh he said,

"Well, well, my men; I guess you will have to dodge the balls. Dodge— but don't run."

In March, 1847, Winfield Scott set out with his force to seize Ve-ra Cruz, which was a large and strong town with a fort on the sea-coast. They had to fight each step of their way through Mex-i-co. They took Cer-ro Gor-do by storm, and at last came to Cha-pul-te-pec, which was built on a rock, and was the great strong-hold of the Mex-i-cans. When this fell all hope was lost, and in the Fall of 1847, our troops marched in the chief town of Mex-i-co, and there put up the Stars and Stripes. In the next year terms of peace were made, which gave us the whole of Cal-i-for-nia and New Mex-i-co.

Who has not heard of Cal-i-for-nia? I will tell you how gold came to be found there.

Some men had been set to work to build a mill-race. As they dug out the trench they saw that the sand was full of bits of stuff that shone like gold. They did not think much of it at first. But as they dug down they found more of it. It was gold! Here in the rock! there in the sand! now in a big lump! now in a small one! It was like a dream! The men were wild! They had but to stoop down and take up this great wealth. The news spread. Young men and old men from the East, and from all parts of the world flocked to the land of gold. Some went by land and some by sea. Some were sick on the way. A host of them died and left their bones where there was no friend to dig a grave. Still the crowds kept on, and some of them were made rich by the gold they found in the strange land. But they had to work hard for it, and lead strange lives; and not all of those who went to Cal-i-for-nia in the year 1849 grew to be rich men. No; some spent all they had, and were poor to the end of their days.

Cal-i-for-nia has grown to be a great State. San Fran-cis-co is its chief town. Gold is still found in the State. Her soil is rich, and her fruits grow to a great size. She has a large trade in wheat, wool, and wine, which are all first-class.

In 1849 the U-ni-ted States made Gen-er-al Tay-lor their chief. In this way they thought to prove their love for, and their faith in him. In less than four months he died, and Fill-more took his place. There was strife here and there through the land, which was brought to an end by wise means, so that no real war took place.

At this time three great men died:—John C. Cal-houn, Hen-ry Clay, and Dan-i-el Web-ster.

Frank-lin Pierce was sworn in as chief in 1853. By this time there was much strife in the North and in the South as the New States came in. There were those who said Kansas should be a free State, and there were those who said she should have slaves. This of course, made a great war of words. It was left for the folks in Kan-sas to say if they would have slaves or not, and then there was a great rush to that State from both sides.

I must tell you now of a man named John Brown who felt that the curse of God was on the land that bought and sold men as slaves. He thought the black man had just as good a right to be free as the white man, and he took the law in his own hands in a rash way. He saw a great wrong and meant to do his best to set it right, with God's help. He could not hope to change the laws of the land, but he was full of fight for a cause so dear to his heart. He took his two sons and went to Kan-sas to help make it and keep it a free State. A few men who thought as he did went with him. He laid up a store of arms, and he and his friends made a way for slaves to get to Can-a-da where they would be free. Brown was a shrewd man, and for some time these things were done on the sly. But some one found out his plans and made them known to those who were his foes.

This roused the wrath of old John Brown, and led him to do in haste what he might have known would hurt his cause. This is what he did. At the town of Har-per's Fer-ry there was a place where a large stock of arms and tools of war were kept. This he made up his mind to seize. His hopes were high. He was sure he should not fail. He went to work with a small force of black and white men ; made the trains stop that here cross the Po-to-mac ; brought work of all kinds to a stand-still, and held the place for more than a day. Most all his men were hurt or slain. His two sons were shot dead. Brown stood by his dead boys, and in a calm voice told his men to stand firm, and sell their lives dear. But the foe was too strong for the brave old man. He was at last caught, tried, and hung ; and the name and fame of John Brown are sung in one of the songs of the land.

This act is known as "John Brown's raid."

CHAPTER XV.

NORTH AND SOUTH AT WAR.

From the year 1857 to 1861 James Bu-chan-an was the chief of these U-ni-ted States. At this time the Mor-mons were at strife with our laws. The Mor-mons think it is right for a man to have more than one wife. They claim to serve God in this way. They make their home in Utah. Their chief town is Salt Lake Cit-y. Troops were sent to quell the strife, but terms were made so that no blood was shed, and so long as the Mor-mons keep the peace we have no law that can touch them. Their mode of life is a great blot on our land.

While Bu-chan-an was chief there was a stir at the South that the men at the North knew not how to deal with. The South said it had a right to keep slaves. Bu-chan-an thought it was wrong, but did not know how to go to work to bring it to an end. Men of wealth who first came from Eng-land to A-mer-i-ca had brought their slaves with them, and their sons were brought up to think that they could own slaves, the same as they owned cows or pigs, and could treat them just as they chose.

Six States cut loose from

the rest. They were U-ni-ted States no more. South Car-o-li-na led them, and they set up as free States; that is, free from the laws that bound them to the North. The bells of Charles-ton rang for joy. Wild shouts of joy were heard in her streets. They chose Jeff-er-son Da-vis to be their chief for the next six years. Those States thought they had the right to do just as they did. All in the South were not of the same mind. The North felt that the States must be kept as one. Those who had gone off must be made to come back by force of arms. Such was the state of our land in the year 1860, when the time came to choose a chief to take the place of James Bu-chan-an.

The choice fell on A-bra-ham Lin-coln. He had been born in the South, but had gone to the west to live when quite a young man. He was tall and gaunt, and had a sad and care-worn face. He took his place on the 4th of March, 1861. At this time Fort Sum-ter, which was off Charles-ton, was the sole fort left in the South where the North had the least foot-hold. It was in charge of a few men with Ma-jor An-der-son at their head.

A large force of troops from the South, led by Gen-er-al Beau-re-gard, had built earth-works from which to fire on the fort. He tried at first to starve out the men in the fort, but word was sent to them that ships were on their way with food.

At dawn of a spring day a bomb-shell went with a whizz through the air and burst on Fort Sum-ter. Its sound went through the land. It was plain there was now to be war. With more men the fort might have been held, for it was strong and well built, but at the end of a day and a half An-der-son was forced to give up the fort. Not a man was hurt.

It had been thought by some that the North would not fight. But she went to work with zeal. Men left their farms, their shops, their trades, their homes, and their dear ones, and were soon in arms and on the way to meet the foe. It was a strange, sad sight.

Both sides thought the war would be a short one.

The first great fight of the war took place at Bull Run. Gen-er-al Scott was too old to take the field, so the troops from the North were led out by Gen-er-al Mc Dow-ell. At first it was thought the North would win, but fresh troops came to the aid of Beau-re-gard, and they broke the ranks of their foes, who set off on a wild run and did not stop till they got back to Wash-ing-ton. This taught the North that it was not a play war.

Lin-coln sent out a call for more men. The whole South was in arms.

Gen-er-al George B. Mc Clel-lan, who had done some good work in Vir-gin-ia, was now made Gen-er-al in chief. He knew how to train troops, but was not the man to lead them in fight.

To tell of all the fights that took place in the long war of four years would make too large a book.

In 1862 the war took a start in the West. A force, led by Brig-a-dier Gen-er-al U. S. Grant, set out in a fleet of gun-boats to take Fort Don-el-son. They laid siege to the fort by land, and by sea, and took it from the hands of the South.

The next great fight in the West was at Shi-loh, on the Ten-nes-see. Grant and Bu-ell led the troops from the North, and Al-bert Syd-ney John-ston and Beau-re-gard the troops from the South. The first shot came from the South, who drove the North down to the brink of the stream. But John-ston was killed; night came on, fresh troops came up to aid the North, and the next day there was a brisk fight, and Beau-re-gard and his men were put to flight.

The next great fight in the west was at Stone Riv-er in Ten-nes-see. It was kept up for three days. There was great loss on both sides, but the North held the field.

At An-tie-tam in Ma-ry-land, a great fight took place, twixt Gen-er-al Lee and Gen-er-al Mc Clel-lan. This was in the fall of 1862. It was hard fought on both sides, and there was great loss of life.

The next fight was in Vir-gin-ia, at Fred-er-icksburg. Burn-side had been put in Mc Clel-lan's place, but he was no match for Gen-er-al Lee, who won the day.

In the spring of 1862 a large fleet of gun-boats, in charge of Ad-mi-ral Far-ra-gut went out to fight the force at New-Or-leans. For six days Far-ra-gut sent shot and shell at the two forts that were in his way, but he could not do them much harm. The foe had put a stout chain from shore to shore so that ships could not get by, and fire-rafts and gun-boats were let loose to do all the harm they could to those that came too near. But Far-ra-gut made his way past forts and gun-boats and took New-Or-leans, which was a great prize.

The South had thought of a new kind of a gun-boat. It was clad in a coat of mail, and did much harm. It was called the Mer-ri-mac. One night there came from New York a strange kind of a craft, which had just been built and was called the Mon-i-tor. There were no masts to be seen. It looked like a cheese box on a raft. There was a fierce fight twixt these two boats, and the steam-ram, the Mer-ri-mac, had to put in to Nor-folk. These sea-fights were kept up for some time, and more gun-boats of the same sort were built in Eu-rope as well as in A-mer-i-ca.

On the first day of the year 1863, Lin-coln did a deed that gave great joy to the black race. He said that from that day all the slaves should be free. Just think of it! The whole North gave thanks to God. The South was not so well pleased, of course, but had to yield to the law.

In May 1863, Gen-er-al Joe Hook-er, who took Burn-side's place, led his troops out to fight Lee's men. They met at Chan-cel-lors-ville in Vir-gin-ia. Lee had but a small force, and Jack-son came up from the South to help him. As Jack-son rode up with his staff he was shot by some of his own men, and had to be borne from the field. He was calm in the midst of great pain. "If I live it will be for the best," he said; "and if I die it will be for the best." He died at the end of eight days, and the death of "Stone-wall" Jack-son was a great grief to the South, and to his friends at the North.

Lee, by his great skill, won the fight at Chan-cel-lors-ville, and Hook-er had to turn back the troops he had sworn to lead "On to Rich-mond." This was a great blow to the North.

The chief fight of the whole war took place at Get-tys-burg, a town in Penn-syl-va-nia. Lee had had such good luck that it made him bold; and his plan now was to march to the North and take Phil-a-del-phia and New York. The North shook with fear at Lee's move, for he had shown great skill.

Gen-er-al Meade was put in Gen-er-al Hook-er's place, and he and a large

THE BATTLE OF GETTYSBURG.

force of troops set out to meet Gen-er-al Rob-ert E. Lee. Meade, though a brave man, felt that he had a hard task. In the first place, the troops were all strange to him; and what was worse than all, they had had such bad luck, that they had no hope in their hearts. But the work had to be done, and he and his men must move at once. "Theirs' but to do and die."

The first fight in Get-tys-burg took place on the first day of Ju-ly, 1863 with the loss of a few men on both sides. At night fresh troops came in for the North and the South, and the fight was kept up all the next day. On the third day Meade held a hill which was full of graves.

Some of the tomb-stones were so old and moss-grown that the names and dates could not be seen. Some of them were fresh and new. The men in gray swore they would take the hill on which Meade and his men were.

The morn of the day on which hung the life, we may say, of the U-ni-ted States, was bright and warm and still. Lee laid his plans to crush his foe at one point. Meade brought his troops to this place where they were to win or lose the fight. At noon all was in trim, and at the sign from Lee's guns a fierce rain of shot and shell fell on both sides. For three hours this was kept up, and in the midst of it Lee sent forth a large force of his men to break through Meade's ranks. Down the hill they went and through the vale, and up to the low stone wall, back of which stood the foe. But Lee's brave men did not stop here. On they went, up close to the guns whose fire cut deep in their ranks, while Lee kept watch from the height they had left. The smoke lifts, and Lee sees the flag of the South wave in the midst of the strife. The sight cheers his heart. His men are on the hill from which they think they will soon drive the foe. A dense cloud of smoke veils the scene. When it next lifts the boys in gray are in flight down the slope where the grass is strewn thick with the slain. Lee's plan did not work well. He lost the fight, and went back to Vir-gin-ia, and as far South as the Rap-id-an.

There was great loss on both sides. For days and days men did nought but dig graves for the dead. For miles round there was not a barn or a house that did not hold men with such bad wounds it was not safe to move them. Some were so hurt and torn that they could not bear the touch of kind hands, but had to lie on the field till death put an end to their pain.

Oh, that there were no such thing as war!

In the spring of 1864 Gen-er-al Grant, who had been put at the head of all the U-ni-ted States troops, left his men at the west in charge of Gen-er-al Sher-man, and took the field to rout Gen-er-al Lee, and to force his way to Rich-mond. There were fierce fights on both sides, and great loss of life. The North had more men and means than the South, and Grant felt that each move he made brought the end more near. His aim was to get Pe-ters-burg and Rich-mond, but not much was done till the spring of 1865. Grant was a man of few words. It is said that "a still tongue shows a wise head." He wrote "I will fight it out on this line," and the North had great faith in him. From the first there had not been a doubt in his own mind but that the North would win. And this gave him strength all through the war. He now felt that he had the foe by the throat, and did not mean to let go his grasp. But for Lee's great skill the war would not have gone on for so long a time.

Let us now turn to the west. At the time that Grant met and fought with Lee in a place known as the Wil-der-ness — May, 1864 — Sher-man had a fight with Gen-er-al J. E. Johns-ton, in Geor-gia, and won his way to At-lan-ta, which was a great gain.

Gen-er-al Hood was now put in place of Johns-ton, and he made up his mind to march to Ten-nes-see and make Sher-man fall back. But in place of this Sher-man gave Gen-er-al Thom-as one half of his force to keep guard in Ten-nes-see, while with the rest of his troops he went through Geor-gia—and oh! what harm was done with fire and sword!—till he came to the sea-coast and took Sa-van-nah. Not a word had been heard from him in a whole month. This is known as "Sher-man's march to the sea," and the fame of it went through the land and made his name great in Eu-rope as well as in A-mer-i-ca.

In the mean time Thom-as had met Hood at Nash-ville and put an end to his whole force.

In Ju-ly, 1864, Ad-mi-ral Far-ra-gut, with a large fleet, went to Mo-bile, which had two strong forts to keep foes at bay. What do you think Far-ra-gut did? He tied his boats in pairs, and then stood in the main-top of his flag-ship, and thus ran the fire of the forts with the loss of but one boat. He had a fight with and took the gun-boat Ten-nes-see, and in a short time, with the aid of a land force, took the two forts and made his way to Mo-bile.

In this year the North met with great loss from gun-boats that were built in Eng-land to cruise the seas and catch or burn all ships that bore the Stars and Stripes. The trade of the North was much hurt, and it was not safe for her to send out ships with rich freight. The Al-a-ba-ma had done the most harm, and in June, 1864, she fought her last fight.

The U-ni-ted States war-ship Kear-sarge came up with the Al-a-ba-ma off the coast of France, and at the end of an hour's hard fight she sank to rise no more. The North knew that Eng-land had built the Al-a-ba-ma for the South and had tried to get the Brit-ish not to let her go to sea. But in spite of this she set sail and did a great deal of harm, for which the North said Eng-land must pay, as she had been to blame. Now when you hear men talk of the "Al-a-ba-ma Claims" you will know what they mean.

In the spring of 1865 it was clear that the South would have to give up the cause for which it had fought for four long years. Gen-er-al Lee still held Rich-mond and Pe-ters-burg. On the first of A-pril Grant sent a force of men to lay siege to the works at Five Forks, where they drove off Lee's men. The next day the whole line of works in front of Pe-ters-burg fell. When Lee found he could not hold Pe-ters-burg or Rich-mond, he took flight with his troops for the west. Grant gave chase and kept close in Lee's rear. At last Lee had to give in. His men were foot-sore and in dire need of food. They could not keep up the fight. Terms of peace were drawn up by Grant, which Lee read and made haste to sign with his name. Then he told how his men had had no food for two days and Grant at once sent them what he could spare. Lee rode back to his troops and in a few words told them what he had done.

"Men," he said, "we have fought, side by side, through the war, and I have done the best I could for you."

By the end of May the South had laid down its arms. The Great War was at an end. The joy was great. All hearts were glad. Flags were at high-mast; bells rang; guns were fired; and at night the streets were bright and gay. In the midst of this joy came the shock of a great grief.

Lin-coln was shot by a bad man named Booth. The deed was done at a play-house in Wash-ing-ton. Booth fled, but was found in a barn, and the shot sent at him was his death wound. Lin-coln died; and grief was deep in the land. Flags are hung at half-mast; the bells that so late rang out a peal of joy, now toll a dirge. Strong men stand in their fields and weep. It is a sad, sad time.

Lin-coln still lives in the hearts of men whom he taught to be firm in the right. He had a warm, true heart, a sound mind, and a strong trust in God who was his help at all times. On the bright roll of fame the name of A-bra-ham Lin-coln stands next to George Wash-ing-ton. One of the few that were not born to die.

CHAPTER XVI.

TIMES OF PEACE AND GROWTH.

It took the North and South some time to bind up the wounds that war had made. The freed slaves had to be set at work. The men who had fought in the war were paid the sums due them, and then they laid down their arms and went back to their homes.

When a chief dies the one next in rank rules, in his stead. The votes of the men of the U-ni-ted States had made An-drew John-son next in rank to A-bra-ham Lin-coln. John-son took his place in A-pril, 1865, the same day that Lin-coln died.

John-son did not go to work right. He made foes both in the North and in the South. He did things that he had no right to do, and broke laws that he should have kept. For this he was tried in 1868, but as his guilt was not proved, he was not put out.

The South came back in 1868 and 1869, and once more all the States from Maine to Cal-i-for-nia were as one.

I have not yet told you of Sam-u-el F. B. Morse, who first taught us how to talk to folks a long way off by means of a wire. The first wire was put up from Bal-ti-more to Wash-ing-ton in the year 1844. Now it seems as if that wire went round and round and round the world, there is so much of it. In 1858 the wire was first put down in the bed of the sea, and in 1866 what was said in New York could be read and known in Eng-land. It was a grand scheme, and there was a great time in all the large towns when the first words were sent through this long wire. What do you think were the first words that were sent through the first wire that was put up? I will put them in big type so that they will stand out on the page. Here they are:

"WHAT HATH GOD WROUGHT!"

Should you go to New York you will find there a brown stone house, in the front of which is set a white stone, on which you may read these words:

"In this house S. F. B. Morse lived for some years; and here he died."

In 1867 the U-ni-ted States bought from Rus-sia a large tract of land known as A-las-ka, for which they paid a large sum in gold. We get fur from there as well as fish.

When John-son's time was out, Gen-er-al Grant was put in his place by a large vote. He soon set things straight, and North and South were on good terms once more. He who had shown his skill in war, had now a chance to bring peace and good will to men. When the time came to choose a chief for the next term, the choice fell once more on Gen-er-al Grant, who took the oath, March 4th, 1873.

There was quite a strife when Grant's friends tried to put him in for a third term, for it was not thought to be a wise plan. So Grant went back to the home-life of which he was so fond, and not much was heard of him for some years.

Then came the sad news that he had lost all his wealth, and was in such ill-health that he must soon die. The best of care could not save him; but he lived on for days and months, and bore his pains as none but a brave man could.

Death was his worst foe, but he was calm through-out the hard fight, and felt no fear.

Grant died Ju-ly 23, 1885; and on Au-gust 8, North and South met as one, and bore the great man to his tomb. The line of march stretched out for miles and miles; and crowds came in by boat and rail to take part in the sad scene.

The show of grief was real, for all hearts felt as if they owed a debt to him, who by God's help, had brought the war to an end.

"Let us have peace!" he cried; and then set to work to bring back peace to the land which had been at strife for more than four years. Grant was great in war, and great in peace, and his name and fame stand with those of Wash-ing-ton and Lin-coln.

But we must now go back to the year 1876 when the U-ni-ted States kept its birth-day. Ten times ten years had gone by since A-mer-i-ca was made free, and the U. S. was born. By this time it was a great strong child. A World's Fair was held at Phil-a-del-phia for six months, to which came crowds from all parts of the world. It was a grand sight; such as one could not hope to see but once in a life-time.

Ruth-er-ford B. Hayes took Grant's place in March, 1877. He was a mild man, and ruled in peace.

In 1881 the choice fell on James A. Gar-field. He was once a poor boy, and had won his way by hard work. He had been through the war, and was much thought of in the West, where he was best known. All the acts of his life show that he was a brave man; and he was so wise and just that he soon had a host of friends.

The warm days came on, and Gar-field left the White House to take the train for New Eng-land. It was good to be free from the cares that had kept him at Wash-ing-ton. He felt like a boy let out of school. He was at peace with all men. He did not think he had a foe in the world. How soon all this was changed! A bad man stood near where Gar-field had to pass, and shot at him as he went by. For long, long weeks Gar-field lay on a bed of pain at the White House. Then it was thought the sea air might help him, so he was borne to Long Branch, where he had the best of care and skill. But all was in vain. He died in the fall of the year 1881, and all men felt that it was a great grief to lose so good and brave a man. Tears fell from the eyes of old and young when the word was sent from Long Branch— "Gar-field is dead!"

Ches-ter A. Ar-thur took Gar-field's place. His rule was a wise and just one, and North and South were at peace. But it was soon time to choose a new man for the White House, and the names of Gro-ver Cleve-land and James G. Blaine were brought to the front, and the claims of each set forth in fine style.

Blaine was a Re-pub-li-can; Cleve-land a Dem-o-crat. Both had hosts of friends, and strife ran high through all the land. Blaine was a fine states-man; for a score of years he had helped make the laws of the U-ni-ted States, and twice be-fore had his friends tried their best to get him in-to the White House for at least one term. But he did not get the votes.

Cleve-land, at this time, was Gov-er-nor of New York State, and had had a chance to show what kind of stuff he was made of. Each good act of his life was made the most of by his friends; each wrong deed was brought to light by his foes, and it was the same way with Blaine. When the votes were cast, Cleve-land won, but did not have much to spare.

Cleve-land was sworn in as Pres-i-dent on March 4, 1885. He was the first Dem-o-crat who had sat in the chair for more than a score of years, and those of his side felt a great joy to see him there.

In Ar-thur's term, a bill had been passed to spend a large sum — $30,000,000 — on new war ships, of which we were in much need ; for the old ones, built for the most part of wood, were out of date. The work on these ships was pushed at a great rate while Cleve-land was in the White House, and aft-er, till we had a grand new na-vy.

On June 2, 1886, Cleve-land took as wife Miss Fran-ces Fol-som. He was the first Pres-i-dent to be wed in the White House.

Near the end of Cleve-land's term there was great strife o-ver the tax which is put on goods that come in to our ports from far lands. This tax was so high that it brought in a sum that there was no use for, and Cleve-land said it ought to be cut down. His side tried to pass a bill to do this, called the Mills Bill, but the Re-pub-li-cans were too strong, and it did not pass. This strife stirred up a great lot of talk a-bout "Pro-tec-tion" and "Free trade," and when the time came once more to choose a chief, not much else was heard of but these things. The Re-pub-li-cans were for Pro-tec-tion, which means that a high tax should be put on all those kinds of goods from out-side that can be made here, so that they will be dear, and the home goods can be sold with-out a cut in the wa-ges of those who do the work, to bring them down to the low rate that is paid in the old lands. Those who are for Free Trade, hold that it is best that all goods should be made where the work can be done at least cost, and that laws should not be passed to make things dear. Cleve-land and the Dem-o-crats were not for out-and-out Free Trade, which means no tax at all, but they were for a low tax.

The Re-pub-li-cans put up Ben-ja-min Har-ri-son, of In-di-an-a, to run a-gainst Cleve-land. He is the grand-son of Will-iam Hen-ry Har-ri-son, the ninth Pres-i-dent. He had served in the war, and been made a Brig-a-dier Gen-er-al, and since then his state had sent him to the Sen-ate. He got more votes than Cleve-land, and was sworn in as Pres-i-dent, March 4, 1889.

There were two small war clouds in Har-ri-son's time. One was raised by a thing that took place in Chi-le in South A-mer-i-ca. Some men from one of our war ships who were on shore were set on, and two were killed. We made a call on Chi-le to pay the wives of the slain men for their loss. Chi-le did not like to do this at first, but at last she did so, and good-will reigned once more.

Then we had some strife with It-a-ly, be-cause some It-al-ians who were in jail in New Or-leans were "lynched;" that is, put to death by a mob with-out a tri-al. Aft-er much talk, we a-greed to pay $25,000 to the friends of the lynched men, and It-a-ly was con-tent.

A new tax bill, called the Mc Kin-ley Bill, was passed in 1890. It made the tax high on goods that can be made here, and pleased those who were for Pro-tec-tion, but the Dem-o-crats found much fault with it.

At the end of four years, Har-ri-son was put up a-gain by the Re-pub-li-cans, while the Dem-o-crats ran Cleve-land for the third time. Cleve-land was the choice of the land, and took the chair once more.

Four hun-dred years had now flown since Co-lum-bus had found the New World, and in hon-or of that great deed a World's Fair was held at Chi-ca-go. It was o-pened May 1, 1893. The grounds were on the shore of Lake Mich-i-gan, and the build-ings put up on them were called the White Cit-y. Here were sent from all parts of the world fine goods, and works of art, ma-chines, tools, boats, cars, fruits, grains, in fact all the things that men make or grow. The build-ings in which they were shown, though not made to last, were as fine in looks as the pal-ace of a king and much more vast, and there were lakes and ca-nals crossed by fine brid-ges. The show went on for six months, and vast crowds came to see it all the time.

For a while in 1895 it looked as if we might have a war with Eng-land. Ve-nez-ue-la, in South A-mer-i-ca, claimed that she was tak-ing some of her land, and called on us for help to stop her, for we have a rule, called the "Mon-roe Doc-trine" that we will let no pow-er of Eu-rope seize land by force on this side of the sea. Cleve-land took a firm stand, and said that Eng-land must not take the land un-less she could show a clear right to it, and that men should be named to look in-to the case, and see just where the line should go. Eng-land at first would not yield to this, but claimed she must her-self be the judge, but in the end she gave in some, and the strife was brought to an end with-out war.

Times were hard and trade poor all through Cleve-land's sec-ond term, and there was much talk as to what was the cause. Most of the Re-pub-li-cans said it was be-cause the Dem-o-crats wished to put an end to the high tar-iff. Cleve-land thought it was from a bill that had been passed in Har-ri-son's time, called the Sher-man Sil-ver Bill, by which a great lot of sil-ver had to be bought and coined. The price of sil-ver had gone down till the weight that is in a dol-lar was not worth more than half a dol-lar in gold. A stop was put to the buy-ing of sil-ver, but things did not mend fast, and then a large part of the Dem-o-crats, who were for sil-ver, turned to be foes of Cleve-land, and there was great strife be-tween those who were for gold, and those who were for sil-ver. The gold men said that we should stick to gold, for it was the coin of all the rest of the world, and the one that did not change in worth, while if we coined sil-ver free for all who brought it, as the sil-ver men wished to do, those who had debts due them, and those who worked for wa-ges, would be paid in dol-lars worth but half their face. The sil-ver men claimed that if sil-ver were coined free, it would soon be worth as much as gold, and that with more coin in the land, trade would grow brisk, and times would be good.

When Cleve-land's time was near out, the Re-pub-li-cans, most of whom were for gold, put up Will-iam McKin-ley, of O-hi-o, for Pres-i-dent, and the Dem-o-crats came out for sil-ver, and put up Will-iam J. Bryan, of Ne-bras-ka.

There were a few Re-pub-li-cans who were for sil-ver, and cast their votes for Bry-an, but there were far more Dem-o-crats who were for gold, and cast their votes for McKin-ley, so he was made Pres-i-dent by a large vote.

Will-iam McKin-ley was born at Niles, in O-hi-o, in 1843. When the war broke out, he went to the front as a pri-vate, and served so well that he rose from the ranks, and at the end of the war was made a Ma-jor. In 1877 he was sent to Con-gress. He had a bright mind, and could speak well, so he made a mark in Con-gress, in which he sat till 1890. He took the chair as Pres-i-dent, March 4, 1896.

CHAPTER XVII.

THE WAR WITH SPAIN.

The isle of Cu-ba, which lies off our coast to the south, had oft been the scene of war 'twixt Spain, which ruled it, and a large part of the Cu-bans, who thought that her rule was not just. The last of these wars broke out in 1895. For three years it went on, and still peace seemed far off, for one side did not get much the best of the oth-er. Spain called home Gen-er-al Cam-pos, who had been her head man in the isle, and sent in his place Gen-er-al Wey-ler. He tried more harsh means to put down the Cu-bans than Cam-pos had used, and in the end it came to pass that a large part of the poor folks in the isle were like to starve to death.

Folks in the U-ni-ted States were much moved to hear of the hard-ships of the

Cu-bans, and not a few said that we ought to f rce Spain to let Cu-ba go free, so that these sad things would come to an end. The Span-iards did not like this talk, and thought that if it were not for the help we gave the Cu-bans they would give up the fight; and so a strong hate for us grew up a-mongst them.

At last a thing took place which brought the ill-will on both sides to a head. On Feb-ru-a-ry 15, 1898, a U-ni-ted States war-ship, the Maine, which had been sent to Ha-va-na to guard the lives and goods of A-mer-i-cans who were there, was blown up in the night, and 259 of the men on board were slain in their sleep. Great was the shock that this gave to all A-mer-i-can hearts, and there was at once a cry for war. To make sure that the ship had not been blown up by chance from the inside, men were sent to look at the wreck, and to talk with those who had been on board, but had not been killed. These men made a re-port that the ship had been blown up from the out-side, and when an end had been thus put to doubt, all minds were made up that Spain must be made to smart for this crime. It was thought that the least that should be done was to force her to give up Cu-ba to the Cu-bans, and a de-mand was made that she do this. She said that she would not, so war was de-clared a-gainst her.

The Pres-i-dent made a

call for troops, and soon the land was all a-stir with men on the march. Camps were formed, and the men be-gan to drill and train for the work they had to do. A large fleet, with Ad-mi-ral Samp-son at the head, was sent to close the ports of Cu-ba, and one not so large, but made up of fast ships, and called a "Fly-ing Squad-ron," with Com-mo-dore Schley in charge, was kept on hand to meet a-ny fleet that Spain might send a-gainst our shores.

The first great fight did not take place in Cu-ba, but off on the oth-er side of the world. When war broke out, Com-mo-dore George Dew-ey, with an A-mer-i-can fleet, was at Hong Kong, in Chi-na. Six hun-dred miles a-way at the Phil-ip-pine Isles, which were owned by Spain, there was known to be a Span-ish fleet. Com-mo-dore Dew-ey got or-ders to find this fleet and fight it. He steamed to Ma-ni-la, the chief town of the isles, and reached the mouth of the bay in which it lies late at night on A-pril 30, 1898. He passed the forts at the bay's mouth with-out hurt, and at dawn next day found the Span-ish fleet at Ca-vi-te, a place near Ma-ni-la where there are forts.

Our ships steamed up in a line, and soon each ship in both fleets was fir-ing each gun it could bring to bear, and the forts were giv-ing what help they could. Com-mo-dore Dew-ey kept his ships on the move, so that they would not make good marks to fire at, and as they passed back and forth, they sent a hail of shots in-to the Span-ish ships that smashed and tore them, and sent death to those on board. The Span-iards fought as brave men, but their aim was wild, and their shots fell wide of the mark.

At the end of two hours the whole Span-ish fleet seemed to be wrecked, and Com-mo-dore Dew-ey gave the word to stop fir-ing, and his ships drew out of range to give the men a chance to rest and eat. At a quar-ter past e-lev-en, they went back, and a few more rounds put an end to the work. The Span-ish ships were all wrecked and sunk, and the Span-ish flag was hauled down from the forts.

On the Span-ish side the killed and wound-ed were 412, while on ours but one was killed and but sev-en got wounds, and no great harm was done to a-ny of the ships. Such great gains with so small a loss had scarce ev-er been known. When the news reached this side of the world, there was a great burst of praise for Com-mo-dore Dew-ey and his men, and all A-mer-i-cans felt proud of the grand deed that had been done. Com-mo-dore Dew-ey was raised to the rank of Ad-mi-ral, and was thanked by the Pres-i-dent and Con-gress.

On A-pril 30, a strong Span-ish fleet, with Ad-mi-ral Cer-ve-ra at the head, put to sea from the Cape Verde Isles, and there was great con-cern to know where it meant to go. All our ships were on the watch to catch the first sight of it. There were a lot of false tales for a while, but at last it was known for sure that Cer-ve-ra had reached the port of San-ti-a-go, in the east end of Cu-ba. Samp-son and Schley both brought their fleets to this place, and lay off the mouth of the bay, to pounce on Cer-ve-ra if he came out. There were strong forts at the mouth of the bay, and mines that would blow up a ship that tried to pass in, or our men would have gone in to fight at once.

To make it hard for Cer-ve-ra to slip out in case a storm should drive our ships a-way, a brave feat was done by Lieu-ten-ant Hob-son. He thought of a plan to sink a ship in the mouth of the bay where it was not wide, so there would be no room to pass. There was small hope that those who did the deed would get off with their lives, for they had to go right un-der the guns of the forts. But though there was need of but sev-en, hun-dreds wished to go. The Mer-ri-mac, a ship that was used to haul coal, was picked out to be sunk; and at 3 o'clock, A. M., June 3d, Hob-son and the brave sev-en set out on their task. A storm of shot and shell from the forts soon fell on them. They brought the Mer-ri-mac to the spot, and then Hob-son fired the bombs on board. He and his men sprang to a small craft they had brought with them, and drifted about in it for a while, till a Span-ish steam launch picked them up and took them on shore as cap-tives. Ad-mi-ral Cer-ve-ra was so struck by their brave deed that he sent word to Ad-mi-ral Samp-son that they were safe, and that he would take good care of them till they could be changed for Span-iards whom we held. When the foe gave such praise to Hob-son, there is no need to say that those of his own land were stirred up to laud him, and that his fame was on all lips.

There had been much doubt as to where in Cu-ba it would be best to strike a blow with the land force, and now that Cer-ve-ra was shut up in the bay at San-ti-a-go, it was thought that that was the right point. So a force of 16,000 troops, with Gen-er-al Shaf-ter in charge, was sent in ships from Tam-pa in Flo-ri-da. On June 22d, the first of these troops were put on shore at a point twelve miles to the east of San-ti-a-go. There was a large Span-ish force in and near San-ti-a-go, and they had done all they could to make the place strong. On each road that led to the town they dug pits in which to stand and fire, and great use was made of barbed wire- a new thing in war. Wires were stretched near the ground to trip up our men as they ran; and at points in reach of the fire of the men in the pits, fen-ces too high to be jumped were put up, so that our men would have to stop and cut them, and thus be good marks to fire at.

It took three days to land all the troops, for it had to be done in small boats. The Span-iards dare not come near the shore to stop the land-ing, as our men-of-war stood off rea-dy to pour out their shot if there was need.

The troops at once be-gan to stretch out their lines to sur-round San-ti-a-g . The roads in those parts are not much more than foot-paths that go through a dense growth of rank brush and plants, and our men had to cut their way through these while the hot sun poured a fierce heat down on them.

A fight took place on June 24th at a post where the Span-iards had a strong force, and in this our troops met their first loss. A-mong those who took part were a troop called Roose-velt's Rough Ri-ders. They came face to face with a Span-ish force that was hid in the tall shrubs, and had all at once to stand a fierce fire. They did not flinch, but pushed on in a brave way, and in the end drove the Span-iards be-fore them, though there were ma-ny more of them.

Some of the Rough Ri-ders were cow-boys from the West, and some were young men who had left lives of ease, and all fought for the flag with great dash and pluck, and at all times had a strong wish to be in the thick of the fight, and to take the lead where there was the most dan-ger. This first fight in which they took part is called the bat-tle of Si-bo-ney.

By June 30th, the A-mer-i-can lines were well spread out to the east of San-ti-a-go, and on Ju-ly 1st a great fight be-gan. The whole line was in the fight, but the main bat-tles took place at the hill town of San Juan, and at El Ca-ney. The Span-iards fought at both points in pits and in stone block-hou-ses that had to be stormed by our men in the face of a hot fire, but they went at them with a dash that swept all be-fore them. The Span-iards made a brave stand, but by night they had been forced from all the posts they had held at the dawn of the day. The next morn they took up posts far-ther back, and the fight went on all this day. Our men had to put up with great hard-ships. Be-sides be-ing all the time un-der fire, they were tired out, and half starved, for not much food had been brought for-ward. By turns they were drenched with rain, or scorched by the sun. A thous-and men had been killed and wound-ed, and ma-ny had to be drawn from the fir-ing line to search for the wound-ed and bear them to the rear.

This state of things, and the fact that his lines were now stretched out so as to be quite thin, made Gen-er-al Shaf-ter think it best not to go on till he could get more troops. So he sent word home that they should be sent on, and in the mean time did not try to do more than hold the ground that had been gained.

When Hob-son sank the Mer-ri-mac in the mouth of San-ti-a-go Bay, he did not take it quite to the spot where it would shut the bay up tight, for the helm was shot off, and it cou!d not be swung round. In a short time the Span-iards found out that, with care, ships could pass through, one at a time. When it be-came plain to Cer-ve-ra that the town was like-ly to fall in-to the hands of the A-mer-i-can land force, he thought he might as well try to break through the fleet that lay on guard out-side, as to wait in the bay. He might get off with some or all of his ships; and if not, it was more brave to be whipped in a fair fight on the o-pen sea, than to wait tame-ly for the foe to come and take them in port.

He made his rush out on the morn-ing of Ju-ly 3d. His ships were four fine, swift, steel-clad cruis-ers, and two craft not so large, called tor-pe-do boat des-troy-ers. They tore out from the bay in a line, and once past the forts, turned sharp to the west. They were seen at al-most the same time by five of the chief ships of our fleet that lay most near to the course they took. One was the Brook-lyn, Com-mo-dore Schley's ship, and the oth-ers were the Or-e-gon, Tex-as, I-o-wa, and In-di-an-a.

Quick as a flash the men were at their posts, and the

guns be-gan to flame and roar, and send out shot and shell thick, as the ships dashed aft-er the fly-ing foe. The Span-ish ships, as they fled, worked all their guns too, and clouds of smoke soon spread o-ver the sea. The Brook-lyn was the most swift of our ships, and took the lead, and on her the Span-iards brought most of their guns to bear, for they thought that if she were stopped they stood a good chance to get a-way. But their aim was poor, while our men sent the shots straight to the mark.

In not much more than an hour from the time they came out of the bay, three of the Span-ish cruis-ers, and both of the des-troy-ers had been wrecked and sunk. The Chris-to-bel Co-lon had got a lead of six miles, and for a time it looked as if she might get a-way. But the Brook-lyn and the Or-e-gon tore aft-er her with speed that grew fast-er and fast-er. and at last came so close they could use all their guns, large and small, on her. With the shells fall-ing thick a-bout her, she ran for the shore and hauled down her flag.

This was the end of the fight, and our men now set to work to try to save the Span-iards from death by burn-ing and drown-ing in their ships. Of the 2300 men who had been on board the Span-ish fleet, 350 were killed, burned, or drowned; the rest were made cap-tives. On our side but one man was killed, and the harm done the ships was slight.

There was not much land fight-ing a-bout San-ti-a-go aft-er this. Gen-er-al Shaf-ter got more troops, and made a call on the Span-ish Gen-er-al, To-ral, to give up the town, or he would have it shelled by the ships, while he made a charge by land. Gen-er-al To-ral would not yield at once, but aft-er much talk, and a few small fights, gave up in the end. On Ju-ly 17th, the Span-ish troops laid down their arms, and the Stars and Stripes were raised o-ver San-ti-a-go, which was to be no more a Span-ish town.

Gen-er-al Miles now went with a force to the isle of Por-to Ri-co, which was al-so owned by Spain. In less than three weeks a large part of the isle was in our hands, with but slight loss of life. Most of the folks in the isle were glad to have our troops come, and cheered our flag when they saw it.

Aft-er Dew-ey had put an end to the Span-ish fleet in the bay of Ma-ni-la, he sent word that though he might shell and des-troy the town with the guns of his fleet, he could not take and hold it with-out a land force. So as soon as they could be got off, troops were sent from our Pa-cif-ic coast, with Gen-er-al Mer-ritt at the head. There were reb-els in the Phil-ip-pines, as in Cu-ba, who wished to be free from the rule of Spain. and these joined in the siege which was laid to Ma-ni-la. There was a fight on Ju-ly 31st, in which the Span-ish loss of life was large, while on the A-mer-i-can side it was but slight. On Au-gust 13th, an at-tack was made at the same time by both the fleet and the land force. Aft-er a fight of six hours, the Span-iards were beat-en. They had to give up the town, and 7,000 Span-ish troops laid down their arms. Our loss in killed and wound-ed was but 50 men.

This was the last fight of the war with Spain, for she had al-rea-dy made a move for peace. On Ju-ly 26th, the French Am-bas-sa-dor, in the name of Spain, had asked Pres-i-dent McKin-ley to say on what terms he would stop the war. In a few days the Pres-i-dent gave him the terms, and on Au-gust 9th news came that Spain would do all that was asked. Word was at once sent to all in charge of our troops to put a stop to the fight-ing. This was be-fore the bat-tle of Ma-ni-la, but the word did not get there till aft-er the fight took place.

Men were named by Spain and the U-ni-ted States to draw up and sign a trea-ty that would make peace between the foes. These men met at Par-is, and there the full terms were fixed. By them, Spain gave up all claim to rule in Cu-ba, and gave to the U-ni-ted States the isle of Por-to Ri-co and the Phil-ip-pine Isles.

CPSIA information can be obtained
at www.ICGtesting.com
Printed in the USA
JSHW081536210623
43541JS00002B/33